THE VEGETARIANS'
HEALTHY DIET BOOK

Colin Spencer and Tom Sanders

Foreword by Professor John Yudkin

*Emeritus Professor of Nutrition
University of London*

GW00506020

MARTIN DUNITZ

To Linda, Mila and Toby

TS

© Colin Spencer 1986

© Introduction by Tom Sanders 1986

First published in the United Kingdom in 1986
by Martin Dunitz Ltd, 154 Camden High Street, London NW1 0NE

British Library Cataloguing in Publication Data

Spencer, Colin
   The vegetarians' healthy diet book: 150
   nutritious recipes.
   1. Vegetarian cookery
   I. Title   2. Sanders, T. A. B.
   641.5'636   TX837

   ISBN 0-94826-905-7

Phototypeset in Garamond by BookEns, Saffron Walden, Essex
Printed by Toppan Printing Company (S) Pte Ltd, Singapore

Front cover photograph shows: Mangetout salad *(top left, see page 57); Millet pilav (top right, see page 82); Broccoli with Maltese sauce (bottom left, see page 97); Stuffed artichoke (bottom right, see page 40).*

Back cover photograph shows: Apple and chestnut tart *(left, see page 114); Syrian fruit salad (centre, see page 110); Melon stuffed with raspberry cream (right, see page 109).*

£1-95

Colin Spencer is one of the best known vegetarian authors in Britain today. He writes a regular column on vegetarian cookery in the *Guardian* and has published a number of vegetarian cookery books, including *Good and Healthy* (published in paperback as *Colin Spencer's Vegetarian and Wholefood Book*) and *Cordon Vert*. He lives in the country and grows many of his own vegetables, ensuring the finest flavours for the vegetarian recipes he develops. He is also the author of nine novels and a talented painter.

Dr Tom Sanders is Lecturer in Nutrition at King's College, University of London, and a recognized authority on vegetarianism. He has researched and written many papers on vegetarian diets. His other special areas of interest are diet related heart disease and young children's diets. He has appeared on a number of radio and television programmes concerned with nutrition, including the recent *World in Action* programme on diet and heart disease.

CONTENTS

FOREWORD

Professor John Yudkin
Emeritus Professor of Nutrition, University of London

The authors of this book on vegetarian diet have not set out to explain or excuse vegetarianism, nor to convert non-vegetarians to a new way of eating. Whatever reasons people have for eating no meat – because they believe it is healthier, or more natural, or more humane, or simply because they dislike meat – it is clearly important that they should not run the risk of dietary inadequacy that might possibly arise from dietary restriction. For this reason, the recipes showing how attractive vegetarian dishes can be are preceded by a general outline of nutritional principles, and specific advice about ensuring good nutrition with vegetarian or vegan diets. After all, foods that are well endowed with essential nutrients have no nutritional value if they are not eaten.

This book thus presents, in a simple and attractive style, the two essential features of healthy eating. First, it tells you enough about nutrition for you to be able to choose the foods that provide a sufficiency of the nutrients that you need. Second, and equally important, it tells you how to prepare these foods in an easy yet pleasing manner so that you will enjoy eating them.

Like other nutritionists, I welcome the present rapid growth in people's interest in finding out more about the relationship between their health and their food. This relationship is excellently expressed in the combination presented in this book of nutritional information and cooking recipes.

INTRODUCTION

There has been a staggering increase in the number of vegetarians in Western countries over the past twenty years so that it is now commonplace to hear people asking for vegetarian food in restaurants, hotels and even aeroplanes. What is often a problem for new vegetarians or their relatives is whether their diet will be adequate. Is there a danger of protein or vitamin and mineral deficiencies? Is there an increased risk of anaemia? Are there any dangers for young children or pregnant and nursing mothers? Although a considerable amount of scientific research has been carried out over the past ten years looking into the diets and health of vegetarians, the answers to these questions have not been easily available. Our intention is to provide a clear guide on how to follow a sound, appetizing and yet simply prepared vegetarian diet. We hope this book will be useful not only to new vegetarians and those trying out vegetarian food part time but also to those who find following their principles among meat eaters sometimes inconvenient, so that they are inclined to rely on snacks of salty cheese or peanuts rather than bother to prepare proper meals.

Why are so many people turning to vegetarianism? There are currently about one million vegetarians in the UK and many more who eat some meals without meat, while fifty years ago the idea was considered cranky and only for religious sects or fringe groups. People decide to give up eating meat for different reasons – for religious or moral convictions, for health, or to support the economic and ecological arguments. Often it seems to be a combination of all these or just a wish to experiment with another way of eating that leads people into vegetarianism. How long they remain vegetarian depends on the strength of their convictions and whether they like the food.

It is easy to choose a diet that is high in fat, salt and sugar – not a recipe for good health. Now that there has been so much publicity about eating healthily, vegetarians need to consider how they should follow the recommended guidelines. In this book we show ways of following a balanced diet that make vegetarian eating both healthy and a pleasure. The recipes each carry an analysis of their calorific, protein, fat, carbohydrate and fibre content. By combining this information with the advice we give here, you can plan attractive and nutritious vegetarian meals.

What are the reasons for being vegetarian?

Most people become vegetarian because they abhor animal suffering and find eating meat repulsive. Many also believe that a vegetarian diet is more natural and wholesome than the typical Western diet and therefore healthier. This idea owes a lot to the food reform lobby who, in the mid-nineteenth century, showed that many foods were over-refined and adulterated with chemicals. Meat products were also often contaminated. They recommended a diet based on wholegrain cereals, fruit, vegetables and fresh milk. The distinction today is of course less clear cut. Because a vegetarian diet is often prescribed by practitioners of alternative medicine, orthodox medical practitioners are sometimes suspicious of the health claims made for vegetarianism.

Another current reason for giving up meat is that a vegetarian diet is more economical when taken in the context of limited food resources which are becoming a worldwide concern. Most of the cereal crop grown in developed countries is used to feed farm animals, yet these cereals could be used directly for human consumption. Producing meat is an inefficient way of feeding people; it takes about 4.5 kg (10 lb) of cereals to produce 0.5 kg (1 lb) of beef. Cereals could be diverted from animal production to feed the hungry in developing countries.

Historically, vegetarianism has strong religious links and this is still the inspiration for a large proportion of vegetarians. In many cultures it was believed that the consumption of flesh would contaminate the mind with thoughts of pleasures of the flesh. This is why vegetarianism has been associated with ascetism and purity of thought. The Hindu and Sikh religions advocate a vegetarian diet, as do certain Muslim and Christian sects. Vegetarianism has also been associated with radical movements, such as pacifism, Fabianism, feminism and animal liberation.

A lot of people are turning vegetarian, if not exclusively at least for a major part of their eating, because of the new attraction of the foods. In the past vegetarian diets were usually monotonous. Now, with changes in communications and food technology, many fruits and vegetables can be bought the year round so that vegetarian diets can be extremely varied.

Different types of vegetarian diet

Vegetarianism covers a broad range of diets. All vegetarians exclude meat and fish; a lactovegetarian includes milk and its products; an ovo-vegetarian includes eggs; an ovo-lactovegetarian diet includes both eggs and milk products; a vegan or strict vegetarian diet contains no food of animal origin whatsoever; a fruitarian diet, which is the most extreme or ultimate form, consists only of raw fruit, nuts and berries.

Usually the first stage in becoming a vegetarian is to give up eating red meat and this is followed by excluding poultry and fish. Some vegetarians give up cows' milk and its products (butter, cheese, yogurt) because they believe that milk production is cruel; calves are taken away from their mothers and are either artificially reared or killed for veal so that the cows' milk can be used for human consumption. Others argue that it was intended for calves not man and so having cows' milk is unnatural. Some vegetarians object to eating eggs for similar reasons. The majority of vegetarians want intensive farming abolished, especially the 'battery' conditions for egg-producing chickens, and those who eat them mostly buy free-range eggs.

Vegans reject all food of animal origin, including milk and its products, eggs, honey and food that has been processed using animal products. Vegans do not use animal products for other purposes. They do not wear fur coats or leather shoes, or use cosmetics which either contain animal products or which have been tested on laboratory animals.

The diet of our ancestors probably consisted mainly of raw fruit, nuts and berries supplemented with the odd insect and small animal. As human beings became civilized they learnt to cultivate plants and how to process certain plants, particularly cereals and root crops, into food. Fruitarians believe people can live on a diet of fruit, nuts and berries and so they exclude grains and processed foods from their diets. Some believe that it is wrong to uproot living plants. Most fruitarians previously have been vegans and most vegans in turn have been vegetarians. Fruitarianism is part of the same philosophy as vegetarianism. Of all the vegetarian diets this is the most likely to be inadequate, as you will see.

How healthy is a vegetarian diet?

A common assumption – already mentioned as one of the reasons for people becoming vegetarian – is that the diet itself is healthier than eating meat. So far this has not been proved scientifically. Conversely, people fear they or their children will become anaemic or underweight. The truth is that the health of vegetarians is very similar to that of meat eaters. There are certainly aspects of the diet which are particularly healthy and those that need to be watched to ensure adequate nutrition. These are explained on pages 14–24.

Several studies have tried to compare the health of vegans and vegetarians with the rest of the population but it is not easy to arrive at a clear answer. Vegetarians often show a different attitude towards health. Many are middle-class and tend not to smoke or drink. How long anyone has been a vegetarian is important, and so are the reasons for choosing to become vegetarian. People who become vegetarians for health reasons obviously bias the results of a study, especially if they started the diet with the aim of curing an illness.

The Seventh Day Adventist church advocates a vegetarian diet and studies of the causes of death of its members have been made in the United States and in Australia. Seventh Day Adventists tend to live longer and have lower rates of death from cancer and heart disease compared with the other people. But they also differ in other ways: they do not smoke, drink tea, coffee or alcohol. Besides, studies of other religious groups, for example Mormons, who do not follow a vegetarian diet and do not smoke or drink, have similarly low rates of cancer and heart disease. This implies that it is not the vegetarian diet that is providing the protection.

Thorough medical examinations made on vegetarians and vegans compared with meat eaters fail to show that they are less healthy or more prone to deficiencies, with the notable exception of vitamin B_{12} (see page 22). Vegans and vegetarians are no more likely to suffer from anaemia than meat eaters. They tend to be lighter than other people of the same height. This is because they carry less fat, which is an advantage since obesity can increase the risk of conditions such as heart disease, gout and diabetes.

Protecting against heart disease
Coronary heart disease is the main cause of death among middle-aged men in the Western world. It is rare in developing countries, where less food of animal origin is eaten, but when people from developing countries begin to eat a Western diet they soon acquire the disease. Several environmental factors have been associated with it – smoking, stress, lack of exercise and diet. It is linked to another condition called atherosclerosis, which may take twenty or thirty years to develop. The arteries become scarred and furred up with fatty material called atheroma, the Greek for porridge.

If one of the coronary arteries that supplies the heart muscle with blood becomes blocked a heart attack is the result. The blockage is often caused by a blood clot. Atherosclerosis increases the risk because it narrows the bore of the blood vessel and provides a rough surface for the clot to stick to. This condition can also affect other parts of the circulation and is probably the main cause of stroke in elderly people. We should all try to reduce the risk of developing atherosclerosis, though clearly the younger you are the more effective prevention is likely to be.

The development of atherosclerosis is strongly linked with high levels of cholesterol, a type of fat, in the blood. Populations with low blood cholesterol levels have less atherosclerosis than those with high levels, and people with very high levels can develop atherosclerosis early and die from a heart attack even before the age of thirty. The level of cholesterol in the blood is affected by genetic and environmental factors. It is the amount of fat eaten that influences blood cholesterol rather than cholesterol in the food. Eggs are particularly high in cholesterol and some people have excluded them for this reason. Yet they have a minor effect compared with a high saturated fat intake. Saturated fats, such as butter and coconut oil, increase blood cholesterol levels and the tendency of the blood to clot, while polyunsaturated fats, such as sunflower seed and corn oil (see pages 15–18) have a weaker but opposite effect.

In the average Western diet, including the lactovegetarian diet, most saturated fat comes from dairy products. Vegan diets contain relatively small amounts of saturated fats and no cholesterol, but plenty of polyunsaturated fats. Blood cholesterol levels are much lower in vegans than either meat eaters or lactovegetarians and are similar to the levels in populations where atherosclerosis is rare. The blood of both vegans and vegetarians clots less readily than meat eaters'. Vegans should be less prone to both atherosclerosis and coronary heart disease than meat eaters or ovo-lactovegetarians. This view is supported by studies on Seventh Day Adventists, which show that the male vegan members have a lower incidence than vegetarian or meat-eating members.

Fibre

One very positive aspect of vegetarian and vegan diets is that they provide plenty of fibre, mainly from cereals, pulses and nuts, but also from fruit and vegetables. Dietary fibre is the structural material, sugars and gums from plants that cannot be digested. It is not a nutrient but provides bulk in the diet and because of its water-retaining properties helps food pass through the gut faster, so that it has a laxative effect. A high fibre intake may offer protection against several diseases of the large bowel and certainly prevents constipation. The richest sources of dietary fibre are bran, peas and beans and wholemeal cereals. Certain types found in oats and pulses (beans, peas and lentils) seem to help control diabetes by slowing down the absorption of sugar into the blood, and most of the more up to date diabetic cookery books include many recipes containing pulses.

One of the side effects of diets high in fibre is flatulence and it has been said that, 'Vegetarianism is harmless enough but apt to fill a man with self-righteousness and wind!' Flatulence is caused by bacteria living in the large bowel producing gases. The amount of gas produced is in proportion to the amount of carbohydrate reaching the bacteria, and a diet high in fibre provides plenty of carbohydrates. Beans are particularly noted for their effects. They contain two sugars, stacchyose and raffinose, that cannot be digested and so combine with the gut bacteria to form gas. Jerusalem artichokes contain a polysaccharide called inulin which cannot be digested, and onions and green pepper also contain fermentable carbohydrates, as well as sulphur-containing compounds responsible for the offensive smell of the emission.

Salt

It is known that high blood pressure is rare in communities with low salt intakes, while in communities with high intakes, this condition is common. High blood pressure is dangerous because it can lead to a blood vessel rupturing in the brain, causing a stroke. Studies of vegetarians show that they tend to take less salt than meat eaters and some, but not all, studies have found that they have lower blood pressures. The cooking hints, see page 31, give advice on cutting down salt in your diet.

Is a vegetarian diet nutritionally sound?

There are good and bad vegetarian diets. Fortunately there are fewer bad diets than good ones and selecting a good diet is simple as long as you avoid the known pitfalls.

The particular questions people turning to vegetarianism ask are: which nutrients are normally provided by food of animal origin; and how can these be replaced by plant food? Food not only provides us with the nutrients we need, but as we have mentioned, may also play an important part in causing degenerative diseases such as coronary heart disease, stroke and large bowel cancer. It is thought that these may result from lifetime exposure to a diet high in fat, salt and sugar and low in fibre. So vegetarians should plan their eating with two objectives in mind: to ensure a good intake of the necessary nutrients, and to minimize this health risk.

The food we eat contains nutrients in different proportions, so the greater the number of good foods in your diet, the greater the variety of nutrients. People who eat only a few foods run the risk of their diet being inadequate. However, even a few foods can make up a sound diet if they are carefully chosen. Vegetarian and vegan diets can easily provide all the nutrients required if the foods are sensibly selected. Fruitarian diets are likely to be nutritionally inadequate and are not recommended (see page 10). Different components need to be considered in building up the right balance:

Energy

Food provides energy for muscular work and for body maintenance. It also contributes to body growth and repair of tissues. Requirements for energy are easily met by vegetarian and vegan diets as long as you eat enough. Calories, or to be more precise kilocalories, are the units used to measure the energy value of food. Calories can be provided by protein, fat, carbohydrates and alcohol. Fruits and vegetables tend to be bulky and provide few calories, so that a diet composed mainly of these foods will be low in calories. This may be desirable if you are an adult trying to lose weight but can be disastrous for a young child who needs plenty of calories. Grains and dairy products, on the other hand, are high in calories and provide the nutrients for growth (the relative nutritional values of some high energy foods are shown in the table overleaf). When planning a vegetarian diet for young children take care not to give a lot of food that is too bulky and make sure enough of the high energy foods are eaten (see page 17).

Protein
In the past a great deal of unnecessary fuss was made about the amount and type of protein in the diet. Only small amounts are needed to provide material for the growth and repair of tissues. Since it cannot be stored in the body a regular intake is needed (see also the table on page 25).

Vegetarians often worry that they are not getting enough protein of the right type. Yet vegetarian and vegan diets almost always provide sufficient amounts. The intake of protein is likely to be inadequate only when sago or cassava are the staple food, but neither of these usually forms a major part of Western vegetarian diets.

Different types of protein
1. High quality protein from milk, soya and eggs is efficiently used by the body and these are convenient sources of protein for the very young, the elderly and the sick. There are now many soya products available, such as tofu (soya bean curd), soya milk and textured vegetable protein. Soya flour can also be used to thicken sauces and in baking.

2. Cereals (wheat, rice, rye, maize, millet, sorghum) and potatoes are most important sources. They contain about 10 per cent of their energy as protein, 10 per cent fat and 80 per cent carbohydrate; they are also rich in fibre. A diet based on these staple foods will ensure an adequate protein intake.

3. Nuts and pulses are rich in protein and when combined with cereals provide high quality protein.

When digested, proteins are broken down into amino acids which are then absorbed – what the body uses are these amino acids rather than protein. Eaten alone, plant proteins, with the notable exception of soya, are not used by the body as efficiently as eggs and milk because they have different amino acid patterns. However, if plant proteins from different sources are eaten together they complement each other and provide high quality protein (for example, baked beans on toast – see also the table on page 17). Even if the plant proteins are eaten at different meals the complementary effect still works.

Fats
Small amounts of fat are needed to provide polyunsaturated fats

	Portion size	Protein (g)	Fat (g)	Fibre (g)
Cereals				
Biscuits, sweet	105 g (10 biscuits)	7	25	2
Bread				
white	215 g (5 slices)	17	4	6
wholemeal	230 g (5 slices)	20	6	20
Flour, wholemeal	150 g (1 cup)	20	3	14
Fruit cake	140 g (3 slices)	7	18	4
Muesli	135 g (1 cup)	17	10	10
Oatmeal, raw	125 g (1 cup)	16	11	9
Rice				
brown	140 g (1 cup)	11	3	6
white	140 g (1 cup)	9	1	3
Nuts				
Almonds	90 g (½ cup)	15	48	13
Brazils	80 g (½ cup)	10	49	7
Hazelnuts	135 g (⅔ cup)	10	49	8
Walnuts	95 g (½ cup)	10	49	5
Pulses				
Beans, dry	185 g (1 cup)	41	3	46
Lentils, dry	165 g (1 cup)	39	2	19
Peanuts	90 g (1 cup)	22	44	7
Soya beans	125 g (1 cup)	42	22	15
curd	715 g (1 lb 12 oz)	53	30	2
milk	660 g (1¼ pt)	15	25	0
Dairy				
Cheese, high fat	120 g (4½ oz)	31	40	0
low fat	520 g (1 lb 2 oz)	71	21	0
Eggs	340 g (6 large eggs)	42	38	0
Milk, skimmed	1515 g (2½ pt)	52	2	0
whole	770 g (1½ pt)	25	29	0
Miscellaneous				
Fats and oil	55 g (2 oz)	0	55	0
Margarine/butter	70 g (2½ oz)	0	66	0
Potatoes	625 g (3 large)	13	1	13
Sugar	130 g (10 tbsp)	0	0	0

Protein, fat and fibre in portions of food providing 500 kcal

and to allow the fat-soluble vitamins such as A and D to be absorbed. Fat also makes food more palatable. Vegetarian and vegan diets often contain much more fat than is necessary for this reason. Most people prefer butter or margarine on their bread to bread alone. However, adding even small amounts of fat can double the calorific value. A slice of bread provides about 80 kcals whereas a slice of bread with butter has about 160 kcals. It is very easy to consume too many calories with a high fat diet.

Protein source	Protein quality*
Egg	100
Human milk	100
Fish	90
Meat	80
Cows' milk	80
Cereal and a pulse (eg, baked beans on toast)	80
Soya beans	75
Potatoes	70
Oatmeal	65
Sesame seeds	65
Cashew nuts	58
Rice (brown or white)	57
Sunflower seeds	56
Peas	48
Lentils	45
Kidney beans	44
Wholemeal bread	40

*Protein score – maximum 100 based on quality of whole egg

Protein quality of some animal and plant foods

A high intake of fat is desirable for very young children as it both provides a concentrated supply of calories and helps in the absorption of fat-soluble vitamins; the natural diet of the human baby, breastmilk, is rich in fat. Diets high in fat are not so good for adults both because they are fattening and they may increase the risk of coronary heart disease in later life (see page 12). It is believed that many heart attacks could be prevented or deferred by reducing the intake of fat, particularly saturated fat. It is recommended that not more than 30 to 35 per cent (70 to 80 g) of the daily energy intake should be from fat and not more than one-third of that should be from saturated fat. The recipes in this book broadly conform to that recommendation. Where the proportion of fat in any recipe is slightly higher, you should balance it out with accompanying low fat foods such as bread, rice or potatoes.

All fats consist of a mixture of different fatty acids. There are three types:

- Saturated
- Monounsaturated
- Polyunsaturated

Fats are categorized according to which fatty acid is predominant. Butter, coconut and palm oils are saturated fats. Olive and rapeseed oils are monounsaturated. Corn, safflower seed, sunflower seed and soya oils are polyunsaturated. Margarine is made from a mixture of animal and vegetable fats but some brands contain vegetable oils only and are labelled accordingly. The blend of oils used in margarine manufacture varies from day to day depending on the market price of the oils. Palm oil is the main vegetable oil used along with soya, rapeseed and sunflower seed oils. Hard margarines (including the vegan variety) are saturated fats just like butter, but so are many of the soft tub margarines, except for those that claim to be high in polyunsaturates. Low fat spreads differ from margarine, containing 40 per cent fat compared with the 80 per cent in margarine. The balance is made up by water.

Nuts and cheese, except cottage cheese, fromage blanc and low-fat quark, have large amounts of fat but are also rich in protein.

The amount of fat supplied by any food depends not only on the amount you consume but also the fat content of the food. For example, milk contains only 4 per cent fat but because a lot is drunk it contributes a large amount of fat to most people's diet.

It is difficult to know how much fat is in a food just by looking at it. Cakes, pastries and biscuits may contain large amounts added during their preparation. The way food is cooked will also affect the fat content; frying especially leads to an increased amount (see also Cooking hints).

Carbohydrates

The cultivated seeds, fruits and roots that contain concentrated supplies of carbohydrates provide the basis of vegetarian diets. Carbohydrates exist in two forms, as starches and as sugars. As a rule fruits are a source of sugar and seeds and roots a source of starches. Digestion breaks the starches down into sugars which are then absorbed.

Starchy carbohydrate foods, such as bread, pasta, rice and potatoes are considered a healthier source of calories than fat or alcohol; they also contain other nutrients in useful amounts. Sugar or sucrose, which is derived from sugar beet or sugar cane, is highly purified and provides no other nutrients. For this reason it has been called a source of empty calories. As well as being a quick way to get fat, eating large amounts of refined sugar leads to tooth decay. Sugar is fermented by bacteria in the mouth and produces acids which can dissolve the enamel of the teeth. There is no need to cut out jam or sugar in cooking entirely or to worry about the small amounts of sugar in prepared foods like baked beans. It is the sugar consumed between meals as sweets, biscuits, cakes and soft drinks that seems to be most harmful. Contrary to the widely held belief, brown sugar, molasses and honey differ very little from refined white sugar nutritionally and so should be used in moderation.

Minerals

A number of minerals are needed in small amounts and can be found in many foods. Some that are essential for health in small amounts are harmful in excess, for example, salt and fluoride. Vegetarians should make sure that they get enough calcium and iron and that they limit their intake of salt.

Calcium is needed to harden bones and teeth. When the body supply is inadequate, bone formation is affected leading to stunted growth in children and bone deformities (called rickets), and osteomalacia (softening of the bones) in adults. These disorders are nearly always caused by vitamin D deficiency and very rarely by an inadequate calcium intake.

Lactovegetarians are likely to get enough in milk and its products but vegans' calcium intakes may be low. Most cereals and staple foods contain very little. Drinking water, especially in hard water areas, may provide some and sesame seeds are another good source. The table below lists other foods with a good supply of calcium. By eating these freely an adequate amount should be available to vegans.

The absorption of calcium is regulated by the amount of vitamin D in your diet but it is also affected by other plant foods. Many plants, for example, rhubarb and spinach, contain compounds called oxalates which react with calcium to form calcium oxalate and this cannot be absorbed by the body. Wheat flour and oats contain phytic acid which interferes with the absorption of several minerals including calcium, iron and zinc. Phytic acid is broken down by yeast so that when wheat flour is made into bread and leavened with yeast the phytic acid is destroyed (see also Cooking hints).

Almonds	50 g/1¾ oz	Milk	
Baking powder	1 g/¼ tsp	cows'	125 ml/¼ pt
Brazil nuts	70 g/2½ oz	human	500 ml/⅔ pt
Broccoli	85 g/3 oz	Molasses	20 g/¾ oz
Cheese		Sesame seeds	10 g/⅓ oz
Cheddar	16 g/½ oz	Soya flour	55 g/2 oz
cottage	200 g/7 oz	Spinach	21 g/¾ oz
Parmesan	10 g/2 tsp	Turnip tops	130 g/4½ oz
Figs, dried	40 g/1½ oz	White bread	140 g/5 oz
Hard water	1 1/2 pt	Wholemeal bread	450 g/1 lb
Haricot beans	70 g/2½ oz	Yogurt, natural	70 g/2½ oz

Portions of some foods providing 125 mg calcium

Almonds	100 g/3½ oz	Mustard and cress	85 g/3 oz
Barley	110 g/4 oz	Oatmeal	85 g/3 oz
Cashew nuts	85 g/3 oz	Pistachio nuts	30 g/1 oz
Curry powder	5 g/1 tsp	Pumpkin seeds	40g/1½ oz
Dark green leafy		Sesame seeds	40 g/1½ oz
vegetables	110 g/4 oz	Soya beans, dry	55 g/2 oz
Haricot beans, dry	55 g/2 oz	Sunflower seeds	55 g/2 oz
Lentils, dry	55 g/2 oz	Wheatgerm	50 g/1¾ oz
Millet	85 g/3oz	Wholemeal bread	140 g/5 oz

Portions of some plant foods providing 4 mg iron

White bread contains more calcium than wholemeal bread, because it is supplemented with calcium carbonate (chalk), and less phytic acid which interferes with calcium absorption. So some people claim white bread is better than wholemeal. At the end of World War II a study was carried out on children in a German orphanage to see if a diet providing plenty of bread, made from white, brown or wholemeal flours, but minimal amounts of milk, would support normal growth. Whatever the type of bread they ate, all the children had a high rate of growth even though some had previously been malnourished. So if plenty of vegetables and wheat of any type are eaten, your calcium intake will be satisfactory.

Iron   A large proportion of the iron in meat eaters' diets comes from meat, especially liver, and many vegetarians worry about becoming anaemic when they first give up meat. Yet this rarely happens, probably because there are plenty of vegetable sources of iron (see the table above).

Iron is needed in small amounts to form haemoglobin, the red oxygen-carrying pigment in the blood. Iron deficiency results in anaemia (low levels of haemoglobin), causing tiredness, weakness and giddiness. From our studies there is no evidence of an increase in the incidence of anaemia among white vegetarians and vegans compared with the rest of the population, and they have also been found to have higher iron intakes, derived mainly from leafy vegetables and unrefined cereals, especially wholemeal bread. On the other hand, anaemia seems to be more common in Asian vegetarians living in Western societies. This may be because their staple food, white rice, contains less iron than wholemeal bread.

How can you ensure a good supply of iron in a vegetarian diet?   Although iron from plant foods is not so well absorbed as iron of animal origin, it is much improved by being combined with vitamin C, which occurs in many fruits and vegetables.

Again, the importance of varying your diet is obvious. Wholemeal bread, pulses, nuts and dark green leafy vegetables are better sources of iron than fruit and starchy foods such as potatoes. Occasionally using a cast iron cooking pot can also boost your iron intake without being harmful.

Vitamins

Vitamins are needed for health in very small amounts because our bodies are not able to manufacture enough of them from other dietary sources. Various disorders such as nightblindness, scurvy and rickets have been known about for centuries but were found only in this century to be associated with a lack of a specific vitamin. Although there are many vitamins, the number of deficiencies that occur naturally is limited.

As the vitamins were discovered, each was first labelled with a letter of the alphabet. Once a vitamin had been isolated and its chemical structure characterized, it was given a name. For example, vitamin A is called retinol. The alphabetic system is still useful because some vitamins appear as a group of different compounds. Vitamin B_{12} exists in several forms: cyanocobalamin, sulphitocobalamin and hydroxycobalamin. It is also useful to refer to the B-complex vitamins (thiamin, riboflavin, niacin, biotin, pyridoxine, folate) as a group because they tend to be found together in the same types of foods such as yeast extracts and wholemeal cereals.

Vitamins are either fat-soluble – A, D, E and K – or water-soluble – the B vitamins and vitamin C. The fat-soluble vitamins can be stored in the body and this means that a regular intake is not essential. It may take several years to deplete the body stores of these. The water-soluble vitamins can be stored for a comparatively short period but even with them it takes several weeks for a deficiency to show.

Are vegetarians in danger of vitamin deficiency? All the vitamins can be provided by foods of plant origin but vitamins D and B_{12} are sometimes lacking in vegan and vegetarian diets.

Fruit and vegetables provide vitamins A, C, E and K, and cereals, grains and nuts the B-complex and vitamin E; so fruit and vegetables complement cereals, grains and nuts to provide a good balance. Vitamin A deficiency is only common among non-meat eaters in parts of the world where people eat very few coloured fruits and vegetables. You could produce a B-complex deficiency by making a refined cereal staple such as white rice too high a proportion of your diet, but this would be easily averted by eating wholegrain cereals or foods rich in the vitamins, such as yeast extract. Refining cereals means that the outer part of the grain which contains most of the B-complex vitamins and the fibre is removed. Most of the vitamins are added back to white flour by bakers when they make white bread. However, wholemeal bread is still better nutritionally than white bread because of its fibre content.

Vitamin D is usually obtained through exposing the skin to sunlight. When sunshine is limited, particularly during the winter months, the amount stored may be insufficient and so extra vitamin D has to be provided in the diet. It is necessary for the absorption of calcium, and vitamin D deficiency causes rickets and osteomalacia (see page 19). The elderly who tend not to go into the sun and young children with high rates of bone growth are vulnerable.

Vitamin D is found in very few foods naturally, mainly fish and liver. However, a synthetic form is added to margarine at a level of 8 micrograms/100 grams. The amount provided by eating margarine is likely to be considerably lower than the recommended 10 micrograms and so it is probably wise to give vitamin D supplements to vegetarian children and the elderly, especially during the winter months.

There is no great risk of rickets or osteomalacia actually developing in white vegetarians but these are common among immigrant Asian vegetarians, probably because of inadequate exposure to sunlight, and unlike the rest of the population, they do not use margarine.

Vitamin B$_{12}$ is the one vitamin most likely to be deficient in vegan and vegetarian diets. It is made exclusively by micro-organisms: cereals, fruits, nuts, pulses, vegetables and other plant foods do not contain it unless contaminated by micro-organisms that produce it, or by insects. Animals cannot make vitamin B$_{12}$ and depend on micro-organisms for it. It is stored in the liver and kidney and so is found in high concentrations in these foods. It is also found in all flesh and dairy foods. Some fermented foods contain B$_{12}$, for example beer and tempeh (soya-bean press cake) but unlike the other B-complex vitamins it is not in wholegrain cereal and yeast extract.

The possible effects of B$_{12}$ deficiency are a type of anaemia, monthly periods stopping (amenorrhoea) and a nervous disorder causing a tingling sensation in the fingers and toes, leading to paralysis. The anaemia can be prevented and cured by another vitamin, folic acid. Since vegans and vegetarians tend to have high intakes of folic acid, because they eat plenty of green vegetables, nuts and unrefined cereals, they rarely have the anaemia associated with vitamin B$_{12}$ deficiency. Consequently, the nervous symptoms, first the tingling and then a loss of sense of touch, are usually the first signs. The deficiency can be remedied with a vitamin B$_{12}$ supplement. If untreated it will progress to cause permanent paralysis and can be fatal. Vitamin B$_{12}$ deficiency can be discovered only by a properly qualified

Beer, draught	600 ml/1 pt
Cheese	
Cheddar	55 g/2 oz
cottage	200 g/7 oz
Egg	1 large
Milk	
cows'	300 ml/½ pt
soya (Plamil)	300 ml/½ pt
Yeast extract	½ tsp
(Barmene,	
Tastex)	

Portions of some foods providing one microgram of vitamin B$_{12}$

medical practitioner after laboratory tests, so you should talk to your doctor if you think there is any danger of this lack in your diet.

The requirement is very small, about one microgram daily and even unsupplemented vegan diets will contain about half a microgram. Vegetarians who eat eggs and milk regularly are likely to have sufficient intakes but vegans may be at risk.

You should have a fairly regular intake (at least three times a week) as you cannot absorb more than about five micrograms in food or pill form at a time. We recommend that lactovegetarians who have only small amounts of milk products (less than 0.25 1/ 10 fl oz milk or 50 g/2 oz cheese daily), as well as all vegans, eat foods supplemented with vitamin B$_{12}$ or take supplements.

The vitamin is produced commercially by growing bacteria on vegetable growth media. This is used to supplement a number of vegan foods, particularly yeast extracts (Tastex, Barmene) and soya milks (Granogen and Plamil). In Britain, all meat substitutes are supplemented with vitamin B$_{12}$ by law. The blue-green algae Spirulina, sold in health food shops, is a very rich source and is acceptable to many vegans although it is not very palatable. Very recently vitamin B$_{12}$ has been added to a number of breakfast cereals, including cornflakes. You can check this by reading the labels on the packets. The amounts of foods providing one microgram of vitamin B$_{12}$ are shown in the table above. The need for vegans to ensure that they have an adequate supply of vitamin B$_{12}$ in their diet cannot be overemphasized.

Are other vitamin supplements necessary? There should be no need for vegans and vegetarians to take any vitamin supplements other than D and B$_{12}$ (except during pregnancy, see page 27). However, many people do choose to take them as an insurance policy. While there is no harm in doing this, there has not yet been any proof that they bring benefits. Because small amounts of vitamins are necessary it does not follow that larger amounts will be better.

Manufactured vitamin preparations should be regarded as medicines and the stated dose should not be exceeded; they should also be kept out of the reach of young children. An excess of water-soluble vitamins is generally not a problem because it can be passed in the urine. But very high doses of many of these vitamins produce drug-like effects, for example, the B vitamin nicotinic acid in large amounts (greater than 80 mg) will lead to flushing which lasts for about two hours, and too much vitamin B_6 can cause neurological disorders. Excessive intakes of fat-soluble vitamins can be more dangerous because they cannot be passed easily in the urine and so accumulate in the body. Too much carrot juice or ß-carotene, which is the provitamin A, makes the skin turn orange. Large amounts of Vitamin A (retinol) cause sickness, headaches and the skin to peel. Deaths have been reported in extreme cases. Vitamin D when taken in excess can cause bone deformities.

How much food do I need?

It is impossible to say accurately how much food any one person needs because everybody's requirements and energy expenditure are different. Therefore, it is only useful to give guidelines on the relative proportions of food in the diet (see the table opposite).

There is no need to plan all the nutrients in the correct proportions. No one eats the same food at each meal day in, day out and any shortfall in one meal should be made up in another. What is important is to make potatoes or a cereal such as bread or rice the basis of your meals, with fruit and vegetables providing complementary nutrients. Generally wholemeal cereals are nutritionally superior to refined cereals, but white bread and white rice are still good foods. The greater the variety in your diet the more you avoid any risk of deficiency. At the same time your food is much more enjoyable. Remember the following points when deciding what foods to provide:

- In the past many vegetarians when they gave up meat and fish compensated by eating more dairy produce and eggs. As the current view is that it is probably healthier to limit the amount of fat, particularly the saturated fat in your diet, it makes sense to be less dependent on milk and cheese and to use plant alternatives.
- You should make sure when cutting down on dairy fat that you maintain your intake of vitamin A. This is easily done by eating a side salad containing leafy vegetables every day with your meals and by eating carrots regularly.
- For the other vitamins aim to eat at least one piece of fresh fruit a day. Oranges and other citrus fruits are particularly rich in vitamin C.
- Wholemeal bread, preferably not spread with butter or

	Men	Women
Energy (kcal)	2400	2150
Protein (grams)	more than 60	more than 54
Carbohydrates (grams)	320–380	290–340
Minimum carbohydrate intake for person on weight reducing diet	100	100
Fat (grams)	40–80	36–72
Ideal fibre intake (grams)	30	30
Calcium (mg)	500	500
Iron (mg)	10	12

Recommended daily amounts of nutrients for adult men and women

margarine, is an excellent accompaniment to soups, vegetable stews and pasta dishes and is particularly nourishing. It is a good idea always to have a generous supply of bread available at any meal.
● A moderate amount of alcohol, a pint of beer a day or a couple of glasses of wine, seems to do no harm and helps many people to relax.

As a rough guide this meal plan, based on our studies of adult vegetarian diets, is very typical and can be recommended:

Breakfast muesli with milk or soya milk
toast with margarine or butter and marmalade
fresh orange juice
unsweetened tea, coffee or tisane
Break coffee, fruit and biscuit
Lunch green salad
wholemeal bread and peanut butter
or baked potato with filling, eg, cottage cheese
piece of fruit
Supper cooked meal with side salad/fresh vegetables
fruit

Weight watching on a vegetarian diet
Ideally your body weight should remain the same throughout adult life. However, most people put on weight as they grow older. Increased weight beginning in middle age is due to an excessive intake of calories for the amount used. You can easily see if you are overweight by standing in front of a mirror without any clothes on. If you can pinch more than 2.5 cm (1 in) of fat

around your waist you are overweight and that will increase the risk of your getting diseases such as heart disease, diabetes or arthritis.

The only proven way of losing weight is to eat fewer calories. This is most easily done by restricting alcohol, fatty foods such as cheese and nuts, and sugary foods such as cakes and biscuits. You can eat as much fruit and vegetables as you like – these provide few calories but a lot of bulk. Cut down on starchy foods such as bread and potatoes as they are fattening in excess, but do not cut them out. Not only are they an important source of protein and vitamins for vegetarians but including a limited amount of carbohydrate in a reducing diet is both safer and more effective.

Try to eat several small meals a day rather than a few large ones and aim to lose weight gradually, at a rate of about 1 kg (2 lb) weekly. Once you have achieved your ideal body weight adjust your food intake so that you neither gain nor lose weight. Weigh yourself regularly, and as soon as you start to put on weight again cut back on what you eat. The recipes in this book give calorie values so you can plan a controlled diet around them.

Pregnancy and lactation

Both pregnancy and lactation proceed quite normally in vegetarian mothers. Pregnancy increases the body's need for nutrients but the body uses them more efficiently so that dietary requirements hardly change. Iron losses are reduced by your periods stopping and iron is better absorbed from the food you eat. Protein is used more efficiently and energy is conserved as fat. The idea that a mother should eat for two is wrong. There is no reason for a woman who is already eating a good diet to change it when she becomes pregnant. Indeed, a woman should be eating a good diet before she even considers becoming pregnant.

There may though be a danger of vitamin deficiency around the time of conception. Vitamin B_{12} and folic acid are essential for cell division and a deficiency of these vitamins is suspected as being the cause of spina bifida. A recent study of high risk mothers found that among those who took multivitamin supplements around conception and during the first few weeks of pregnancy there were fewer spina bifida babies than among those who did not.

The foetus gets its supply of oxygen from the maternal blood and anaemia will retard its growth. So many doctors prescribe iron and folic acid tablets to mothers (vegetarian and meat eaters) during pregnancy as a safeguard against anaemia. Supplementing your diet with iron during pregnancy also means that your baby will be born with greater stores of iron.

During pregnancy, women lay down a considerable amount of body fat, usually about 4 kg (9 lb). This is an entirely natural process and happens to all mammals. The fat acts as an energy store to help subsidize lactation. Each kilogram of fat deposited during pregnancy can be cashed in during lactation to yield 9000 calories, which is sufficient to support the cost in energy of producing 10 litres (16 pints) of milk. Mothers who put on a lot of fat while they are pregnant do not need to eat as much during lactation as those who put on very little. Two pieces of advice if you are pregnant or breastfeeding: do not attempt to diet; if you feel ravenously hungry, eat more.

The amount of breastmilk you produce is affected by your diet to some extent but also by your hormones and psychological factors. If you do not produce enough milk it is generally due to these factors rather than an inadequate diet. The vitamin content of your breastmilk, though, is definitely affected by your diet. If you have a vitamin deficiency it can only mean your baby will too. A few years ago a very severe case of vitamin B_{12} deficiency was discovered in a baby breastfed by a vegan mother who had not been taking vitamin B_{12} supplements. The deficiency in the baby was treated by giving his mother B_{12} supplements. We have measured the levels of vitamins in the breastmilk of vegans and vegetarians and have found low levels of vitamin B_{12} in the milk from those mothers who did not take supplements or eat foods containing the vitamin. Women who either took supplements or ate food supplemented with vitamin B_{12} had levels in their breastmilk similar to meat eaters.

Vegan and vegetarian mothers must make sure they have a source of vitamin B_{12} in their diet; but we have usually found higher levels of the other vitamins in the breastmilk of vegetarians and vegans than in the milk of meat eaters.

Feeding the vegetarian baby

Most vegetarians and vegans breastfeed their babies well into the second year and then wean them on to their respective diets. These children's growth and development are normal but there is a tendency for them, especially the vegans, to be shorter and lighter than average. Although no baby should be grossly underweight under the age of five years, there is no evidence that being smaller than average is harmful; it may even be an advantage. A gradual slow growth rate is more likely to prolong life.

Breastmilk is the best food for the human baby, providing all the nutrients necessary for at least the first six months and, under optimal conditions, up to a year. The supply begins soon after the baby is born. The more quickly the baby is put to the breast after birth, the more likely lactation is to be successful; and the more a breast is suckled the more milk it will supply. So demand feeding is best. The amount of milk babies take varies greatly. Some babies thrive on 600 ml (1 pint) and others need 1 litre (1¾ pints) to maintain the same rate of growth. Usually babies take between

600 and 700 ml (1 to 1¼ pints) per day in the first three months. The best way of knowing whether your baby is getting enough milk is to check the weight gain. Most babies gain 110 to 140 g (4 to 5 oz) a week in the first three months and by the age of six months they should have doubled their birth weight.

If your supply of breastmilk is inadequate infant milks based on a modified cows' milk formula can be used. There are special soya infant milks, such as Velactin and Granolac, which were developed for feeding babies who could not tolerate cows' milk. These soya milks should be used only as complementary feeds for babies under six months. Never use them as the sole source of food for any length of time without consulting your doctor. After six months, once your baby has started taking other food, you can use soya milks freely.

Weaning foods such as puréed fruit and vegetables and baby cereals and rusks can be introduced at six months. The aim is to get your baby used to the idea of accepting food other than milk. When you begin to give more solids wholemeal bread is good to start with, spread with margarine and smooth peanut butter or a yeast extract. Do not fill your baby up with bulky and watery foods like puréed green vegetables and fruit – these are not sufficiently concentrated forms of nutrition. Make sure that the food is smooth and does not contain bits that could lead to choking; never give unground nuts to young children.

Beyond the age of one, your baby should be introduced to the food the rest of the family eats. Make sure that the meals provide a mixture of a pulse and a cereal for high quality protein, for example, baked beans on toast or rice and lentils. Additional milk will not be necessary if your baby is breastfed, but some type of whole milk (and this can be soya milk) is needed in the human diet up until the age of two. Do not use skimmed milk to feed your child under the age of five unless you give rich sources of vitamin A, such as carrots and greens, regularly.

Children brought up as vegans need vitamin D drops such as Adexolan from the age of six months, but do not exceed the stated dose. As long as your baby is breastfed, vitamin B_{12} supplements are not necessary if your intake is adequate. Nevertheless, it is a good idea to use foods containing B_{12}, such as soya milks and yeast extracts, during weaning.

After five
From now on there is no need for special food. The balanced vegetarian diet you eat yourself will also supply what is necessary for your child's growth and development. The quantities children eat vary from one to another by as much as several hundred calories per day. As long as your child is growing steadily without becoming overweight, you should not be unduly worried about calorific intake.

Vegetarian parents have to remember that as children get older you are less able to regulate what they eat. Eating is an important part of social life besides providing nutrients. Vegetarian children will often eat what they like in other children's houses. It is probably more important to allow them to mix socially than to insist on their adhering strictly to vegetarian principles.

The recommendations in this book are for a balanced diet that will sustain a hungry teenager as well as a fully grown adult. The quantities needed will be in line with what you'd expect to give any adolescent – up to twice as much as you might eat yourself. It would be encouraging for a lone vegetarian in the household sometimes to cook the recipes in this book for the whole family.

COOKING HINTS

Here are the ways to get the best nutritionally from your vegetarian diet, as well as to achieve better textures and flavours in the foods.

Retaining the vitamins
Food preparation can greatly affect the vitamin content:

- Boiling causes some of the water-soluble vitamins to be leached out into the cooking water, and if it is thrown away they will be lost.
- Prolonged cooking and exposure to air destroys riboflavin, folate, vitamin B_{12} and vitamin C.
- Some vitamin C is destroyed if food is chopped up and left for several hours exposed to air before it is eaten.
- Vitamins are lost when vegetables are cooked and then kept warm for several hours before being eaten.

The best way to conserve vitamins in vegetables is to chop them up immediately before use, cook them in a minimum of water and serve them as soon as they are cooked. Prepare salads as near the time they are eaten as possible.

Preserving food can lead to vitamin losses. Most of the vitamin C is lost when fruit and vegetables are canned or bottled, although many manufacturers now put vitamin C back into the food. Freezing is usually the best preserving method with only minimal losses. It also retains fresher flavours.

Fats
To cut down on your intake of saturated fats:

- Use cottage cheese or quark in place of full fat cheese
- Skimmed, semi-skimmed or soya milk in place of whole milk
- Low-fat yogurt in place of cream
- Olive, safflower or sunflower seed oil in place of hard fats
- Either a low fat spread or a margarine high in poly-unsaturates instead of butter or ordinary margarine
- Avoid rich cakes and short biscuits.

Frying   Using a Chinese wok greatly reduces the amount of fat in cooking. Its convex shape means only a little is needed for light frying.

Baking (vegan)   Recipes in this book using butter, such as tarts and pies, can be equally successfully cooked with one of the hard vegan margarines (Tomor, Mapleton's Nutter). The nutritional analyses will be the same.

Salad dressings   Aim to use very little oil in dressings, and introduce the fresh flavours of herbs such as basil, mint and marjoram, and lemon juice, or flavoured vinegars.

Breadmaking
The longer you leave your bread to prove the more phytic acid in the bread will be broken down by the yeast. This will make the minerals in your diet more available (see page 19).

Pulses
Dried beans must never be eaten raw after soaking, unless sprouted, as they contain natural toxins. These poisonous substances are destroyed after boiling for ten minutes. For red kidney beans rapid boiling for the first ten minutes is essential. For other types, the water must reach boiling point for at least ten minutes during the cooking. Do not use a slow cooker for beans, since the water never reaches boiling point.

Peas, beans and lentils will cook more quickly if salt is not added during cooking. Most beans take 1½ hours to cook in an open pan or 30 minutes in a pressure cooker. Lentils are best cooked in an open pan and take about 20 to 30 minutes to cook. The red or Egyptian lentils are the fastest cooking and don't need soaking.

Salt
Most of the salt we eat is added to our food at the table or during preparation and cooking and, as there are no positive advantages to eating larger amounts than necessary, it is best to avoid adding salt during cooking and at the table season a prepared dish as lightly as possible. Although the taste of food may first appear bland you can soon adapt, and will find the flavour of freshly cooked vegetables much more subtle. The salt occurring naturally in foods such as cheese will give you enough for your body's needs.

Yeast extracts contain large amounts of salt but are extremely valuable to the vegetarian in other ways, providing B-complex vitamins. Because they are used in small amounts, they make only a small contribution to the total salt intake.

Measurements
The measurements are given in both metric and imperial units.

Use one system only; do not combine them.

Where spoonfuls are referred to, level spoons are meant unless otherwise stated.

1 tsp (teaspoon) = 5 ml
1 tbsp (tablespoon) = 15 ml

To ensure success, check the size of the spoons you are using. Australian users should remember that as their tablespoon has been converted to 20 ml, and is therefore larger than the tablespoon measurements used in the recipes in this book, they should use 3 x 5 ml tsp where instructed to use 1 x 15 ml tbsp.

Vegan recipes
These are marked with the symbol Ⓥ for easy reference. Others including milk, margarine or butter can be adapted substituting vegan margarine and soya milk. These are marked thus: (V).

APPETIZERS

Perhaps the highest intake of unhealthy food that the majority of us consume comes from eating snacks made commercially – the easily accessible junk food. It is not difficult to alter this trend completely by making enticing food, which can be used for parties, or enjoyed instead of a first course.

Beans contain a high quota of fibre and they also purée beautifully. Their bland earthy taste can be given zest with the addition of spices, herbs and flavoured oils and vinegars. Wholemeal bread can be cut in ways to make croûtes or croûtons, and there is also a variety of vegetables which can be stuffed; contrary to Shirley Conran's famous dictum, there is more than enough time to stuff a mushroom, tomato or egg.

As croûtes fried in the traditional way are too high in fat for the recommended diet, you can always smear the bread with oil and let them crisp in a hot oven for a few minutes.

Croûtes I $\boxed{V}$

Per croûte: 90 kcal/2 g protein/5 g fat/10 g carbohydrate/ negligible fibre

1 wholemeal French loaf   *olive oil*
6 cloves garlic

Cut the loaf into 5 cm/2 in slices. Cut out a circle in the middle of each slice of about 2.5 cm/1 in deep, leaving a rim of about 1.5 cm/½ in all around the side. Fry the garlic in the oil. Remove the garlic, then smear the croûtes lightly with the oil. Bake in a hot oven until crisp and browned. Drain on absorbent paper and fill the centre hole with any of the purées below.

Croûtes II $\boxed{V}$

Per croûte: 90 kcal/2 g protein/5 g fat/8 g carbohydrate/ 2 g fibre

1 large wholemeal loaf   *olive oil*
6 cloves garlic

Slice the bread as for toast and either cut each piece diagonally into 4 or cut each piece into 4 squares. Fry the garlic in the oil. Remove garlic then smear the croûtes lightly with the oil. Bake in a hot oven until crisp. Drain on absorbent paper and use as a base for any of the purées or fillings below.

Fromage frais

Total recipe: 400 kcal/13 g protein/37 g fat/5 g carbohydrate/
2 g fibre

145 ml/5 fl oz fromage frais, low fat   *2 drops Tabasco*
quark or Greek yogurt   *seasoning*
1 bunch spring onions, finely chopped

Place all ingredients in a bowl and mix thoroughly. Serve chilled.

Ricotta spread

Total recipe: 670 kcal/28 g protein/60 g fat/5 g carbohydrate/
1 g fibre

225 g/8 oz ricotta cheese   *2 tsp green peppercorns*
60 ml/2 fl oz low fat quark   *seasoning*
1 onion, finely sliced, or 2 shallots,
finely sliced

Mix all ingredients into a paste and chill before use.

Caribbean bean purée   Ⅴ

Total recipe: 650 kcal/31 g protein/32 g fat/63 g carbohydrate/
35 g fibre

140 g/5 oz dried black beans   *1 tsp ground cumin*
2 tbsp walnut oil   *1 tsp ground coriander*
55 g/2 oz grated ginger root   *seasoning*

Soak the beans overnight. Drain, boil fiercely in clean water for about 10 minutes, then drain again and throw away the water. Heat the walnut oil in a large pan and add the ginger root and spices. Let them sweat in the oil for a minute or two, then add the beans and enough water to cover them by about 5 cm/2 in. Bring to the boil and leave to simmer for 1½ hours or until the beans are tender. Drain, but retain the liquid.

Place the beans and seasoning in a blender and whizz, adding enough of the cooking liquid to obtain a smooth purée.

Flageolet purée

Total recipe: 870 kcal/32 g protein/55 g fat/66 g carbohydrate/
36 g fibre

140 g/5 oz dried flageolet beans   *2 bay leaves*
60 ml/2 fl oz olive oil   *2 tbsp Greek yogurt*
1 tbsp summer savory   *seasoning*
zest and juice of 1 lemon

Soak the beans for a couple of hours then drain them. Heat the
olive oil in a pan and add the summer savory, the beans and the
zest and juice of the lemon. Let them cook for a moment, stirring
the pan, before adding enough water with the bay leaves to cover
the beans by about 5 cm/2 in. Bring to the boil and simmer for 1½
hours or until the beans are tender. Drain, retaining the cooking
liquid.

Place the beans in a blender with the rest of the ingredients and
whizz, using enough of the liquid from the beans to obtain a
smooth purée.

Humous   Ⅴ

Total recipe: 1010 kcal/34 g protein/62 g fat/85 g carbohydrate/
26 g fibre

170 g/6 oz chick peas   *4 cloves garlic, crushed*
zest and juice of 2 lemons   *55 g/2 oz fresh mint, finely chopped*
2 bay leaves   *juice of 1 lemon*
2 tbsp olive oil   *seasoning*

Soak the chick peas overnight. Drain, then place in a pan with the
zest and juice from the 2 lemons, the bay leaves and enough water
to cover by 5 cm/2 in. Bring to the boil and leave to simmer for at
least 2 hours. Drain, but save liquid. Discard the zest and bay
leaves.

Place the chick peas in a blender and add the olive oil, garlic,
mint, extra lemon juice and seasoning. Add enough of the liquid
the peas were cooked in to achieve a smooth purée.

Mangetout purée   (V)

Total recipe: 300 kcal/11 g protein/21 g fat/18 g carbohydrate/
13 g fibre

450 g/1 lb young mangetout   *seasoning*
25 g/1 oz butter or margarine

Remove any fibrous parts from the mangetout and cook them in
a little water until they are tender. Place in the blender with

butter and seasoning and whizz until you have a smooth purée. Chill before use.

Brussels sprout purée $\boxed{V}$

Total recipe: 780 kcal/26 g protein/54 g fat/51 g carbohydrate/ 23 g fibre

450 g/1 lb Brussels sprouts
85 g/3 oz brown breadcrumbs
zest and juice of 1 lemon
2 tbsp walnut oil

¼ tsp grated nutmeg
2 drops Tabasco
seasoning

Cook the sprouts in a little boiling salted water for about 5 minutes or until they are just tender. Drain them well, then place in a blender with the rest of the ingredients and process until you have a thick purée. Chill before use.

Bobines de fromage   See photograph, page 50

Total recipe: 455 kcal/14 g protein/44 g fat/1 g carbohydrate/ negligible fibre

170 g/6 oz ricotta cheese
1 tbsp low fat quark
½ tsp each of the following spices:
  paprika
  curry powder
  cumin
  green peppercorns
  cinnamon
  turmeric

For decoration:
pine nuts
pistachio nuts
walnuts
dried fruit

Mix the ricotta and quark thoroughly. Divide the mixture into 6 and roll into thimble shapes. Cover each one with one of the spices and decorate.

Gruyère puffs

Total recipe: 1245 kcal/60 g protein/80 g fat/76 g carbohydrate/ 11 g fibre

145 ml/5 fl oz water
25 g/1 oz butter
½ tsp salt
½ tsp cayenne pepper

115 g/4 oz wholemeal flour
4 eggs
170 g/6 oz Gruyère cheese, grated

Preheat the oven to 200°C/400°F/gas 6. Oil a baking sheet.

Boil the water with the butter, salt and cayenne pepper in a saucepan. When it is bubbling, pour in the flour in a steady stream, stirring all the time until the mixture leaves the sides of the pan. Remove from the pan and let it cool a little. Beat the eggs together. Slowly add the eggs to the cooled mixture, beating continuously. When the eggs have been absorbed by the dough, add most of the cheese, saving a little to sprinkle over the puffs while they cook.

Place tablespoons of the dough on the oiled baking sheet, leaving about 5 cm/2 in between each one. Sprinkle each puff with a little of the remaining cheese, then bake in the oven for 45 minutes until golden brown. Serve hot.

Falafel

Total recipe: 1120 kcal/56 g protein/48 g fat/123 g carbohydrate/ 41 g fibre

225 g/8 oz dried chick peas
1 tsp baking powder
2 large onions, finely chopped
6 garlic cloves, crushed
1 tsp each:
  ground coriander

cumin
fennel seed
1 bunch fresh parsley, finely chopped
seasoning
2 egg whites
2 tbsp corn oil for shallow frying

Soak the chick peas overnight. Drain, then boil for 2 hours. When tender, drain again and crush the peas to a powder in the liquidizer. Pour the crushed peas into a mixing bowl and add the rest of the ingredients except for the egg whites and corn oil. Mix thoroughly, then taste to check seasoning. Beat the egg whites until they are stiff, then fold them into the mixture.

Heat the corn oil in a frying pan and drop in small spoonfuls of the mixture, about the size of a walnut. Don't overcrowd the pan. Let them brown on all sides, then drain on absorbent paper. Falafel are best eaten warm.

Potato and sesame falafel

Total recipe: 1590 kcal/30 g protein/109 g fat/138 g carbohydrate/ 10 g fibre

675 g/l lb 8 oz mashed potatoes
3 tbsp sesame seed paste
2 tbsp roasted sesame seeds

2 egg whites, whipped
seasoning
2tbsp corn oil for shallow frying

Mix all the ingredients together and fry small portions of the mixture in the hot oil. Best served warm.

Potato fingers

Total recipe: 1685 kcal/47 g protein/95 g fat/171 g carbohydrate/
13 g fibre

675 g/1 lb 8 oz mashed potatoes   *1 egg, beaten*
85 g/3 oz Cheddar cheese, grated   *seasoning*
85 g/3 oz wholemeal flour   *2tbsp corn oil for shallow frying*

Mix all ingredients together into a smooth dough. Cut small
pieces off lump of dough and roll into small fingers. Fry in the hot
oil. Best served warm.

FIRST COURSES

The best and most healthy first course is always crudités, with or
without a selection of purées. Any of the purées throughout
this book can be used and, in this section, I have indicated a
variation whereby instead of presenting the crudités on a large
central platter, the cook arranges a few on individual plates with
an avocado sauce.

I have mainly avoided high fat cheeses and been cautious in the
use of eggs, as both these ingredients can be over used in
vegetarian first courses. I have also omitted the most obvious first
courses, which are the seasonal ones that we most enjoy and which
we tend to eat in the simplest way. It is unnecessary to give recipes
for the first asparagus, artichokes and sweetcorn. The golden rule
for eating well and healthily is to have fresh and simple dishes.

Many of the tarts and quiches on page 64–70 can also, of course,
be eaten as first courses. Instead of one or two large tarts, you
make individual tartlets.

Crudités with avocado sauce

Total for the avocado sauce: 1495 kcal/40 g protein/136 g fat/30 g
carbohydrate/12 g fibre

selection of vegetables in season   *zest and juice of 1 lemon*
fresh herbs for garnish   *2 cloves garlic, crushed*

For the avocado sauce: *285 ml/½ pt low fat yogurt*
2 large avocados   *seasoning*

Choose 3 or 4 different vegetables, such as celery, carrots, mushrooms, cauliflower and peppers. Prepare and trim them. Set aside. Peel and stone the avocados. Place the flesh in a blender with the zest and juice of the lemon, the garlic, yogurt and seasoning. Blend until you have a smooth sauce. Arrange small portions of the fresh vegetables on individual plates. Pour a little of the sauce on to each plate and garnish with a fresh herb.

Avocado with onion and green peppercorn sauce [V]

Serves 4
Per serving: 410 kcal/7 g protein/41 g fat/4 g carbohydrate/4 g fibre

2 cloves garlic, crushed	*1 bunch spring onions*
zest and juice of 1 lemon	*crisp lettuce leaves*
2 tbsp olive oil	*2 large avocados*
seasoning	*2 tbsp green peppercorns*

Mix the crushed garlic, lemon zest and juice with the olive oil. Season. Chop the spring onions and mix them with the dressing. Arrange the lettuce leaves on 4 individual plates. Peel and cut the avocados in half, removing the stones. Slice each avocado half lengthways several times, ensuring that you keep the pear shape. Place 1 avocado half on each plate. Pour over the dressing and scatter the peppercorns over each portion.

Pears with guacamole [V]

Serves 4
Per serving: 260 kcal/4 g protein/24 g fat/8 g carbohydrate/3 g fibre

2 avocados	*2 tomatoes*
1 small onion, chopped	*seasoning*
2 cloves garlic, crushed	*4 William pears*
zest and juice of 1 lemon	*a few lettuce leaves*
2 tbsp olive oil	*1 tbsp green coriander, chopped*
1 fresh green chilli	*for garnish*

Slice the flesh from the avocados into the blender jar. Add the onion, crushed garlic, zest and juice of the lemon, and the olive oil. Blend to a purée. Carefully deseed the green chilli and chop finely with the tomatoes. (Do not touch your face or eyes with the chilli juice on your fingers. Rinse your hands after chopping the chilli.) Add the chilli and tomato to the avocado with the seasoning and blend again.

Just before serving, pile the guacamole into the centre of a large platter. Peel the William pears and slice them in half. Arrange them around the guacamole, lightly pressed into the purée. Garnish with a few lettuce leaves and sprinkle the chopped coriander over the top.

Stuffed artichokes

See photograph, page 50

Serves 4

Per serving: 80 kcal/6 g protein/negligible fat/14 g carbohydrate/ 25 g fibre

4 large globe artichokes
400 g/14 oz can hearts of palm
145 ml/5 fl oz low fat yogurt
zest and juice of 1 lemon

2 cloves garlic, crushed
generous bunch chives, finely chopped
seasoning
1 tbsp soy sauce

Trim the tops off the pointed leaves of the artichokes. Boil the artichokes in plenty of salted water for 45 minutes. Drain well and leave to cool. Next, take out the central leaves, leaving a wall of outside leaves. Dig the hairy chokes out of the artichokes, leaving the pad of flesh at the base intact. Discard the hairy chokes.

Take the leaves you have removed and, with a sharp knife, scrape the edible part from the base of each leaf. Drain the can of hearts of palm and dice the flesh, adding it to the rest of the artichoke flesh in the bowl. Mix in the yogurt, lemon zest and juice, crushed garlic and chives. Stir well, taste and season.

Pile the mixture into each of the prepared artichokes. Just before serving, dribble a little of the soy sauce over each one.

Stuffed courgettes

Serves 4

Per serving: 115 kcal/11 g protein/3 g fat/12 g carbohydrate/ 5 g fibre

4-6 medium size courgettes
1 medium size onion
285 ml/½ pt cottage cheese

1 tbsp French mustard
seasoning
parsley sprigs for garnish

Trim the ends of the courgettes and slice them in half lengthways. Scoop out the seeds in a boat-shaped indentation from each half and lay them inside downwards until the stuffing is ready. Chop the onion finely and add to the cottage cheese with the mustard and seasoning. Mix thoroughly. Fill the courgettes with the mixture, pressing the stuffing down firmly and pressing the sides of the courgettes inwards around the stuffing. Chill for 1 hour then cut into 1 cm/½ in slices and arrange on a platter. Garnish with the parsley sprigs.

Stuffed peppers

Serves 4
Per serving: 320 kcal/11 g protein/29 g fat/5 g carbohydrate/ 3 g fibre

2 green peppers	*285 ml/½ pt cottage cheese*
2 red peppers	*2 tbsp capers*
1 bunch spring onions	*2 cloves garlic, crushed*
1 generous bunch parsley	*seasoning*
55 g/2 oz Roquefort cheese	

Cut the tops from the peppers and carefully core and deseed them. Set aside. Finely chop the spring onions and the parsley. Crumble the Roquefort into the cottage cheese and add this mixture to the onions and parsley. Then add the rest of the ingredients and mix thoroughly. Fill each of the peppers with the stuffing. Do this very carefully and ensure that the stuffing is pushed right down to the bottom of each pepper. Chill for an hour, then slice the peppers across in 1 cm/½ in chunks and arrange on a platter, alternating red with green.

Stuffed tomatoes

Serves 4-6
Per serving: 110 kcal/8 g protein/4 g fat/12 g carbohydrate/ 5 g fibre

2-3 large marmande or beef tomatoes	*2 cloves garlic, crushed*
(allow ½ tomato per person)	*1 bunch basil, finely chopped*
55 g/2 oz wholemeal breadcrumbs	*seasoning*
25 g/1 oz grated Parmesan	*25 g/1 oz Gruyère, grated*
1 tbsp tomato purée	

Preheat the oven to 200°C/400°F/gas 6.

Cut the tomatoes in half. Scoop out the seeds and juice, leaving the exterior flesh intact. Place the tomato pulp in a bowl and add all the rest of the ingredients, except the Gruyère. Mix thoroughly. Fill the tomato halves with the stuffing and sprinkle each one with grated Gruyère. Bake in the oven for 10 minutes. These may be served hot or cold.

Lettuce rolls

Makes 12 rolls
Per roll: 50 kcal/4 g protein/4 g fat/1 g carbohydrate/negligible fibre

12 large lettuce leaves
1 ripe avocado
285 ml/½ pt cottage cheese
2 cloves garlic, crushed

1 bunch spring onions, finely chopped
handful mint, finely chopped
seasoning

Blanch the lettuce leaves in boiling water for a moment or two. Carefully drape the leaves over a colander to drain. Peel and stone the avocado and chop the flesh into the jar of a blender. Add the cottage cheese and the crushed garlic and blend to a thick purée. Turn the mixture out into a mixing bowl and add the finely chopped onions, mint and the seasoning. Mix thoroughly.

One by one, lay the lettuce leaves flat and place about a tablespoon of the stuffing at the end of each leaf. Roll up the length of the leaf, tucking in the sides as you go, until you have a small lettuce parcel. Chill for 1 hour before serving.

Spinach rolls

Makes 12 rolls
Per roll: 90 kcal/7 g protein/6 g fat/2 g carbohydrate/1 g fibre

12 large spinach leaves
285 ml/½ pt cottage cheese
55 g/2 oz Gruyère, grated
55 g/2 oz Parmesan, grated
2 cloves garlic, crushed

1 tsp paprika
55 g/2 oz broken walnuts
25 g/1 oz wholemeal breadcrumbs
seasoning
a little butter

Preheat the oven to 175°C/350°F/gas 4.

Blanch the spinach leaves in boiling water for 1-2 minutes, then drain the leaves carefully over the sides of a colander. Mix the 3 cheeses together with the garlic and paprika. Add the broken walnuts and the breadcrumbs. Season to taste.

One at a time, lay out the spinach leaves and place a tablespoon of the stuffing mixture on the end of each one. Roll up the length of the leaf, taking care to tuck in the sides as you go, until you have a small, neat spinach parcel. Place the spinach rolls in an ovenproof dish, dot with butter, cover with foil and bake in the oven for 20 minutes. The rolls can be eaten hot, warm or cold.

Spinach pâté (V)

Serves 4
Per serving: 170 kcal/12 g protein/13 g fat/2 g carbohydrate/10 g fibre

55 g/2 oz butter or margarine	*pinch grated nutmeg*
910 g/2 lb leaf spinach	*seasoning*
zest and juice of 1 lemon	

Melt the butter or margarine in a saucepan and add all the spinach leaves. Place a lid over the pan and simmer for 10-12 minutes or until the bulk of the spinach is reduced by two-thirds. Add the lemon zest and juice, the nutmeg and seasoning. Liquidize in a blender. Pour into individual ramekin dishes and place in the refrigerator for 1 hour to set.

Spinach and apricot mousse

See photograph, page 50

Serves 4–6
Per serving for four: 320 kcal/26 g protein/16 g fat/17 g carbohydrate/18 g fibre

115 g/4 oz dried apricots	*145 ml/5 fl oz low fat yogurt*
675 g/1 lb 8 oz spinach	*4 eggs*
55 g/2 oz Parmesan, grated	*seasoning*
55 g/2 oz Gruyère, grated	*a little butter*

Soak the apricots overnight and cook them gently in their own liquid for 10 minutes. Boil fiercely to reduce the liquid. Leave to cool. Preheat the oven to 200°C/400°F/gas 6. Cook the spinach leaves in their own juice for 10-12 minutes or until the bulk of the spinach has reduced by two-thirds. Leave to cool, then place the spinach in a liquidizer with 25 g/1 oz of Parmesan and 25 g/1 oz of Gruyère. Add half of the yogurt and 2 of the eggs. Blend and season and pour into a mixing bowl. Now put the apricots in the liquidizer and add the remaining cheese, yogurt and eggs. Blend.

Butter a terrine, mould or bread tin and line it with greaseproof paper. Butter the paper then pour in some of the spinach mixture to a depth of about 2.5 cm/1 in. Next, spoon over a layer of the apricot mixture. Continue alternating the layers in this way until the dish is full. Place in a baking tin with boiling water almost up to the top of the mould, cover the top with buttered paper and bake in the oven for 1 hour or until a knife dipped into the centre of the mousse comes out clean. Let the mousse cool thoroughly before turning it out. Because of the greaseproof paper lining, it will unmould with ease. Turn out on to a platter, peel the paper away and garnish with sprigs of parsley.

Tempura vegetables

Total recipe for batter: 350 kcal/8 g protein/30 g fat/13 g carbohydrate/2 g fibre

Selection of prepared mixed vegetables,
chosen from:
  mushrooms, cauliflower, celery,
  fennel, onions, courgettes
oil for deep frying

For the batter:
2 tbsp wholemeal flour
1 tbsp plain flour
½ tsp salt
2 egg whites
3-4 tbsp water

Prepare the vegetables by slicing them into bite-sized pieces.
Make the batter by sieving the flours together and adding the salt. Beat in the egg whites. Gradually add the water to the mixture. Heat the oil until smoking. Dip the pieces of vegetable into the batter then deep fry them. They should be cooked within 2-3 minutes. Drain them well before serving.

Tapénade

Total recipe: 670 kcal/11 g protein/68 g fat/5 g carbohydrate/10 g fibre

225 g/8 oz black olives, stoned
55 g/2 oz capers
1 green chilli, deseeded and chopped
1 tbsp soy sauce

2 tbsp olive oil
juice of 1 lemon
freshly ground black pepper
yolks of 2 hard-boiled eggs

Place all the ingredients, except the egg yolks, into the jar of the blender and liquidize to a thick purée. Pile the purée into the centre of a large platter and crumble the egg yolks over the top.
Serve surrounded with pieces of hot brown toast or wholemeal pitta bread.

Piperade

Serves 6
Per serving: 140 kcal/6 g protein/11 g fat/5 g carbohydrate/2 g fibre

3 large peppers
2 large onions
2 large courgettes
3 tbsp olive oil

450 g/1 lb tomatoes
seasoning
4 eggs

Core and deseed the peppers and chop them coarsely. Chop the onions and courgettes. Heat the oil in a shallow pan and add the chopped peppers, onions and courgettes. Sauté over a low heat for 20 minutes, by which time all the vegetables should be soft and beginning to merge into each other. Remove the skin from the tomatoes before adding them to the pan. Cook for a further 10 minutes or until the vegetable mixture has become a rough purée. Season and then add the eggs, stirring and scrambling them into the mixture. Serve immediately.

Faiscedda

Serves 4
Per serving: 150 kcal/12 g protein/7 g fat/10 g carbohydrate/ 5 g fibre

450 g/1 lb broad beans, podded
1 tbsp summer savory, finely
  chopped
4 eggs, beaten

145 ml/5 fl oz low fat yogurt
seasoning
a little butter

Preheat the oven to 200°C/400°F/gas 6.
  Boil the podded beans in a little water until they are tender – about 10 minutes. If the beans are old, the outside skins will have to be removed after they have been boiled. Place the beans in a blender jar with the rest of the ingredients except the butter and liquidize.
  Lightly butter 4 ramekin dishes and distribute the mixture evenly between them. Bake in the oven for 12-15 minutes, or until all of the faiscedda have risen. Serve with more yogurt if desired. Faiscedda are also delicious eaten cold.

SOUPS

Good healthy soups are the easiest dishes to make in the whole of the cook's repertoire. However, there are a few important general rules to observe.
  First, make sure that the ingredients are in prime condition. The vegetables should be as fresh as they possibly can be for intensity of flavour and the maximum mineral and vitamin content. It is nearly always best to sauté the prepared vegetables in a little fine quality olive oil (buy extra virgin first pressing, if you can get it).
  Stock is the next important ingredient and though it is probably easier to use vegetarian stock cubes you will find that the kitsch flavour of packet soups is creeping into your home cooking. For

the stronger flavoured soups made with pulses and winter vegetables no stock is necessary, but when it is needed, the best stock can be made from celery, onion and garlic. You chop a whole head of celery with two onions and simmer them with various optional flavourings – bay leaves, parsley or garlic. Let the mixture simmer for 45 minutes and crush the vegetables with a potato masher. Leave to cool, then strain the stock from the vegetable debris. This liquid will keep, bottled in the refrigerator, for a couple of weeks. Alternatively, you can make a good stock using the outside leaves of any green vegetable you have – cabbage, Brussels sprouts, cauliflower – chopped up with onion and carrot. Season and simmer in 1.15 1/2 pt of water for 30 minutes. Blend in the liquidizer, then sieve.

Soups can often be helped at later stages of cooking with the addition of a little of one of the following: walnut or hazelnut oil, a good soya sauce like shoyu or tamari, flavoured vinegars like tarragon, basil or shallot. It is important to remember that no recipe book can give you a blueprint with precise amounts to ensure the exact mixture of flavours at the end. As with all cooking, tasting and checking flavours is the key to success.

Soups can be a delicious and satisfying meal in themselves when eaten with wholemeal bread.

Tomato soup $\boxed{\text{V}}$

Serves 6

Per serving: 60 kcal/2 g protein/negligible fat/7 g carbohydrate/ 3 g fibre

1.35 kg/3 lb fresh tomatoes
145 ml/5 fl oz dry sherry or vermouth

seasoning
1 tbsp fresh basil, chopped (optional)

This is simplicity itself to make.

Puncture the tomatoes and place them in a saucepan with the sherry or vermouth and seasoning. Cover with a close fitting lid and place over a very low heat. Leave for about 10-15 minutes by which time the tomatoes should have cooked, mainly in their own juices, and will now be reduced a pulp. Let them cool before placing them in a blender. Liquidize, then strain the soup through a sieve. Throw away the tomato debris and reheat the soup, adding the chopped fresh basil, if you have any, at the last moment.

Garlic soup   Ⅴ

Serves 6
Per serving: 225 kcal/3 g protein/19 g fat/12 g carbohydrate
3 g fibre

3 heads of garlic	*seasoning*
3 tbsp best olive oil	*3 slices wholemeal bread for croûtons*
1.7l/3 pt water	*olive oil for frying*
pinch of saffron (optional)	*2 tbsp finely chopped parsley*

Break the garlic cloves from the heads and place in a bowl. Cover them with boiling water and leave for 3 minutes. They will now peel easily. If the cloves are big, cut them in half.

Heat the olive oil in a pan and add the garlic cloves. Let them cook in the oil for a few minutes before adding the water, the saffron if you have any, and the seasoning. Let the soup simmer for 1 hour. Allow it to cool, then pour into the blender to liquidize the garlic completely.

Cut the wholemeal bread into small cubes and fry until crisp and brown in olive oil. Reheat the soup and pour into warmed bowls. Divide the croûtons equally between the bowls and sprinkle with the chopped parsley before serving.

Beetroot and ginger soup I

Serves 6
Per serving: 95 kcal/3 g protein/5 g fat/10 g carbohydrate/
2 g fibre

55 g/2 oz ginger root, peeled and grated	*1 onion, peeled and chopped*
2 tbsp olive oil	*2.3l/4 pt water*
450 g/1 lb raw beetroot, peeled and chopped	*seasoning*
	145 ml/5 fl oz low fat yogurt

Cook the grated ginger in the olive oil for a moment or two, then add the chopped beetroot and onion with the water. Bring to the boil and simmer for 2 hours. Leave to cool then liquidize in the blender. Return to the pan, season and reheat gently. Check the seasoning before serving and allow each person to add the yogurt to their own bowl of soup.

Beetroot and ginger soup II

Serves 6   See photograph, page 49
Per serving: 65 kcal/4 g protein/negligible fat/12 g carbohydrate/
6 g fibre

450 g/1 lb raw beetroot, peeled and chopped	*1 small white cabbage, chopped*
	5 cloves garlic, crushed

55 g/2 oz ginger root, peeled and   seasoning
*   grated   145 ml/5 fl oz low fat yogurt*

Preheat the oven to 175°C/350°F/gas 3.

Put the chopped vegetables with the garlic and ginger into a large casserole dish. Season and pour boiling water over all the vegetables so as to cover them by about 4 cm/1½ in. Place the casserole in the oven and allow to cook slowly for 2½-3 hours.

Take the dish from the oven and pour off the liquid. You should have a clear red liquid with an intense and delicious flavour. Discard the vegetables, as all their goodness has gone into the stock. Serve the soup with yogurt. This is a thin soup, but none the worse for that.

Fennel and orange soup   Ⅴ

Serves 4
Per serving: 125 kcal/4 g protein/negligible fat/23 g carbohydrate/8 g fibre

2 fennel roots   1 small glass (20 ml/1½ fl oz) ouzo
6 oranges   or anise
2 cloves garlic, crushed   seasoning

Cut the feathery leaves from the fennel roots and reserve. Grate the rest of the roots into a bowl and cover with boiling water, leave until cool. Reserve 1 orange and squeeze the juice from the other 5. Add the garlic and orange juice to the fennel. Grate the zest from the remaining orange and add that to the bowl of fennel, then peel the orange carefully, ensuring that all the pith comes off. Slice the orange across thinly and float in the bowl. Next add the anise or ouzo and seasoning. Stir well and chill thoroughly for 1 hour. Pour into a soup tureen and decorate with the chopped fennel leaves.

Carrot soup   (V)

Serves 6
Per serving: 60 kcal/1 g protein/4 g fat/6 g carbohydrate/ 4 g fibre

25 g/1 oz butter   1.7l/3 pt water
675 g/1 lb 8 oz carrots, washed, 1 tbsp raspberry vinegar
*   trimmed and chopped   seasoning*

Beetroot and ginger soup II (*above*, see page 47), Fennel and orange soup

Melt the butter in the saucepan, add the chopped carrots and let them cook for a moment or two, then add the water and simmer for 30 minutes or until the carrots are done. Let the soup cool and then liquidize to a purée, adding the raspberry vinegar and seasoning.
This soup is an excellent source of vitamin A.

Chilled sorrel soup

Serves 6
Per serving: 75 kcal/5 g protein/4 g fat/5 g carbohydrate/ 4 g fibre

225 g/8 oz sorrel leaves
25 g/1 oz butter
1 large onion, chopped
seasoning

1.7l/3 pt celery or vegetable stock (see page 46)
285 ml/½ pt Greek yogurt

Tear the sorrel leaves from their stalks. Melt the butter in a saucepan and add the leaves and onion. Season and cook slowly with the lid on for 5 minutes. Add the vegetable stock and simmer for a further 10 minutes. Leave to cool, then reduce to a thin purée in the blender with the addition of the yogurt. Check for seasoning. Chill for an hour before serving.

Note: Sorrel is highly astringent in its flavour which is not dissimilar to gooseberries.

Chilled avocado soup   Ⅴ

Serves 4
Per serving: 580 kcal/14 g protein/47 g fat/27 g carbohydrate/ 3 g fibre

2 large ripe avocados
juice and zest of 1 lemon
1 clove garlic, crushed

seasoning
1.45 1/2½ pt unsweetened soya milk

Peel and stone the avocados and cut up the flesh into the blender jar. Add the lemon juice, zest, garlic and seasoning. Liquidize, gradually adding the soya milk, to obtain a thin purée. Chill for 1 hour before serving.

Stuffed artichoke (*top*, see page 40), Spinach and apricot mousse (*centre*, see page 43), Bobines de fromage (*bottom*, see page 36)

Hot avocado and green pepper soup (V)

Serves 4
Per serving: 395 kcal/7 g protein/39 g fat/4 g carbohydrate/
4 g fibre

2 large ripe avocados
1.7l/3 pt vegetable stock (see page 46)

2 large green peppers
25 g/1 oz butter or margarine
seasoning

Peel and stone the avocados and cut the flesh into the blender jar.
Add half the stock and liquidize.
    Core and deseed the peppers and slice them thinly. Cook them
in butter or margarine in a covered saucepan for 5 minutes then
add the other half of the vegetable stock and simmer for a further
10 minutes. Leave to cool before liquidizing the peppers to a
thin purée.
    Now mix the avocado and pepper purées together, season and
reheat gently in a saucepan. Do not let the soup boil – the avocado
must not cook.

Cream of green pea soup (V)

Serves 6
Per serving: 160 kcal/12 g protein/5 g fat/18 g carbohydrate/
4 g fibre

the heart of a cos lettuce
450 g/1 lb fresh peas, podded
25 g/1 oz butter
570 ml/1 pt water
1.15l/2 pt skimmed milk or unsweetened soya milk

seasoning
85 g/3 oz tofu (available from Chinese or health food stores)

Chop the lettuce heart and cook this with the peas and the butter
in a pan for a few moments before adding the water. Let the
mixture simmer for 15 minutes, then allow to cool. Add the milk,
seasoning and tofu. Liquidize the soup to a thin purée. Reheat
gently.
    In summer this soup may be served well chilled.

Thick split pea soup (V)

Serves 6
Per serving: 135 kcal/6 g protein/6 g fat/15 g carbohydrate/
3 g fibre

140 g/5 oz dried split peas
25 g/1 oz butter

1 tbsp olive oil
2 onions, chopped

3 cloves garlic, crushed   1.7 l/3 pt celery stock (see page 46)
2 bay leaves   seasoning

Soak the split peas overnight and drain them well. Melt the butter with the olive oil in a saucepan, add the chopped onion, garlic and bay leaves. Let them cook for a moment or two then pour in the celery stock and add the split peas. Bring to the boil and simmer for 1 hour. Allow to cool and then liquidize to a smooth thick purée. Season and reheat the soup.

Haricot bean soup   (V)

Serves 6
Per serving: 200 kcal/13 g protein/4 g fat/29 g carbohydrate/ 16 g fibre

340 g/12 oz dried white haricot   *2 tbsp olive oil*
* beans*   *3 cloves garlic, crushed*
1.7l/3 pt water   *1.45l/2 pt celery stock (see page*
225 g/8 oz onions   * 46)*
225 g/8 oz French beans   *seasoning*
25 g/1 oz butter

Soak the beans overnight then cook in the water. They should be tender within 2 hours, but check, for they may need a little more water as they are cooking. Meanwhile, chop the onions and French beans. Heat the butter and oil in a pan, add the crushed garlic, the onions and French beans. Cook for a moment before adding the celery stock. Simmer for 20 minutes.

Pour half the haricot beans, with their liquid, into the blender and purée until smooth. Mix the purée with the rest of the beans and then add the rest of the vegetables and their stock. Reheat, stirring carefully. Taste for seasoning before serving.

Green winter soup   (V)

Serves 6
Per serving: 150 kcal/10 g protein/4 g fat/20 g carbohydrate/ 12 g fibre

225 g/8 oz dried flageolet beans   *1.7l/3 pt vegetable stock (see page*
1 small green cabbage   * 46)*
25 g/1 oz butter   *seasoning*
4 cloves garlic, crushed   *1 generous bunch parsley*

Soak the flageolet beans for a few hours then simmer them for 1 hour or until they are tender. Meanwhile, chop the cabbage, melt the butter in a saucepan and add the cabbage and garlic. Leave to cook gently in the butter for 5 minutes before adding 1.45 1/2½ pt of the vegetable stock, then simmer for 20 minutes. Drain the cooked beans and add them to the vegetable mixture. Season to taste.

Pour the remaining 285 ml/½ pt of vegetable stock into a blender and add the parsley, removing the stalks first. Liquidize to a green purée and add this to the soup. Reheat, stirring with care.

Spinach soup

Serves 4
Per serving: 330 kcal/15 g protein/25 g fat/11 g carbohydrate/ 7 g fibre

450 g/1 lb leaf spinach	*570 ml/1 pt unsweetened soya milk*
25 g/1 oz butter	*seasoning*
85 g/3 oz sage Derby cheese, grated	
1.15l/2 pt vegetable stock (see page 46)	

Tear the spinach leaves from the stalks and discard stalks. Cook the leaves in the butter in a covered saucepan over a low heat for 5 minutes Add the cheese and the vegetable stock and simmer for a further 5 minutes. Leave the soup to cool, then blend into a thin purée, adding the soya milk and the seasoning. Pour back into the saucepan and reheat gently.

Note: If you cannot find sage Derby, use any hard cheese such as Cheddar and add a pinch of sage.

Macaroni and bean soup   Ⓥ

Serves 6
Per serving: 310 kcal/15 g protein/9 g fat/45 g carbohydrate/ 16 g fibre

225 g/8 oz dried haricot beans	*1 tsp oregano*
3 tbsp olive oil	*1 tbsp tomato purée*
1 onion, finely chopped	*225 g/8 oz wholemeal macaroni*
2 cloves garlic, crushed	*seasoning*
1 head celery, finely chopped	*vegetable stock (optional)*
1 tsp ground rosemary	

Soak the haricot beans overnight, then cook them in plenty of water until they are tender, which will be about 2 hours. Place half of the beans in a blender and liquidize, adding enough of the cooking liquid to obtain a purée.

Heat the olive oil in a pan and cook the onion, garlic, celery, rosemary and oregano over a low heat for 5 minutes. Add the beans in their water, the tomato purée and the macaroni. Simmer for 10 minutes. Season. Now add the liquidized beans and reheat gently, stirring well. If the soup is too thick, add some vegetable stock to achieve a good consistency.

SALADS

Almost any vegetable can be eaten raw: chopped, diced, grated and occasionally blanched, then tossed in dressing. Not only are vegetables delicious raw, they also retain all the essential nutrients which are so often lost in cooking. The old days of a salad being a few tired lettuce leaves with sliced tomato and cucumber are dead and gone except, sadly, in some catering. Salads can now be made from a large range of vegetables in season, combining them with fresh and dried fruits, nuts, grains and pulses.

To achieve successful salads the first essential is to buy the very freshest of ingredients. If you have a garden there is no problem and we all know that leaves picked in the kitchen garden, then immediately dressed and tossed in a salad, have a density of flavour which is never apparent in leaves bought in the market.

For salad enthusiasts there is now a greater range of salad vegetables on the market. Radicchio, purslane, Italian chicory and batavia can all be found in markets and these, as well as many more delicious and unusual vegetables, can be grown in our gardens.

Even if these more obscure vegetables are out of your reach, you can still make exciting salads from the vegetables which are in season. In my view, a salad of raw vegetables eaten once a day is good for health. Many salads can be summer meals in themselves and many of the winter salads would also make a tempting light lunch.

Green salad

Serves 4
Per serving: 80 kcal/2 g protein/8 g fat/1 g carbohydrate/ 2 g fibre

1 cos lettuce
handful dandelion leaves
1 bunch watercress
1 bunch parsley
2-3 sorrel leaves

1 tbsp lemon juice
2 tbsp walnut oil
1 tbsp low fat yogurt
seasoning

Arrange all the lettuce leaves around the sides of a large bowl. In the centre place the dandelion leaves, watercress and the parsley, without stalks. Tear the sorrel leaves from their stalks and sprinkle the leaves over the centre of the bowl. Mix the lemon juice, oil, yogurt and seasoning together. Pour this dressing over the centre of the salad just before serving.

Spinach, sorrel and avocado salad

Serves 4
Per serving: 355 kcal/10 g protein/32 g fat/8 g carbohydrate/
9 g fibre

225 g/8 oz young spinach leaves   *zest and juice of 1 lemon*
115 g/4 oz young sorrel leaves   *2 tbsp walnut oil*
2 ripe avocados   *seasoning*
2 cloves garlic, crushed   *55 g/2 oz pistachio nuts*

Wash and trim the spinach and sorrel leaves, cutting away any stalks that look too fibrous. Arrange the leaves around the sides and bottom of a large salad bowl. Peel and stone the avocados. Slice them into another bowl and add the crushed garlic, zest and juice of the lemon, walnut oil and seasoning. Just before serving, pile the avocado with its dressing into the bottom of the salad bowl. Sprinkle the pistachio nuts over the top.

Pepper salad $\boxed{\text{V}}$

Serves 4
Per serving: 95 kcal/2 g protein/8 g fat/4 g carbohydrate/
2 g fibre

2 green peppers   *zest and juice of 1 lemon*
2 red peppers   *2 tbsp olive oil*
2 yellow peppers   *seasoning*
1 tbsp fresh lovage, chopped   *handful nasturtium flowers (these are*
handful nasturtium leaves, chopped   *edible)*
1 tbsp green peppercorns

Core and deseed all the peppers. Slice them finely but keep the colours separate. Take the largest platter you have and sprinkle the base with half of the lovage and nasturtium leaves. Arrange the green, red and yellow peppers in strips across the platter. In a bowl mix the green peppercorns with the lemon zest and juice. Add the oil and seasoning and stir well. Pour the mixture over the sliced peppers. Now sprinkle the other half of the lovage and nasturtium leaves over the peppers. Decorate with nasturtium flowers.

Note: Some people might prefer to wear dark glasses while eating this salad as it is a riot of blazing colour!

Tomato and basil salad

Serves 4
Per serving: 105 kcal/2 g protein/8 g fat/7 g carbohydrate/
4 g fibre

910 g/2 lb tomatoes
generous bunch fresh basil leaves
1 tbsp red wine vinegar

2 tbsp olive oil
seasoning

Slice the tomatoes thinly and arrange evenly in a large shallow dish. Chop the basil coarsely and cover the tomatoes with it. Mix the rest of the ingredients and pour over the top just before serving.

Courgette salad

Serves 4
Per serving: 115 kcal/2 g protein/8 g fat/9 g carbohydrate/
4 g fibre

910 g/2 lb young courgettes
1 bunch mint, chopped
1 tsp lemon juice

2 tbsp olive oil
seasoning

Trim and grate the courgettes into a large salad bowl. Add the rest of the ingredients and stir well.

Mangetout salad ⊻

Serves 4
Per serving: 280 kcal/9 g protein/9 g fat/44 g carbohydrate/
8 g fibre

225 g/8 oz roasted buckwheat (see method)
450 g/1 lb mangetout
1 bunch spring onions

zest and juice of 1 lemon
2 tbsp olive oil
seasoning

Buckwheat can now be bought already roasted. If you manage to find some, follow the instructions on the packet. If the buckwheat is unroasted, place a little oil in a heavy pan and heat until very hot. Add the buckwheat and cook, stirring all the time, until it becomes crisp, brown and nutty.

Empty the roasted buckwheat into a large bowl. Trim the mangetout and slice in half. Blanch in boiling water for 1 minute. Chop the spring onions coarsely. Add the mangetout and onions to the buckwheat. Add the lemon zest, juice and oil. Season and mix thoroughly.

Note: Buckwheat is also sold as bulgar wheat or cracked wheat.

Mushroom, onion and walnut salad   Ⓥ

Serves 4
Per serving: 162 kcal/4 g protein/ 15 g fat/3 g carbohydrate/
4 g fibre

450 g/1 lb mushrooms	*1 tbsp red wine vinegar*
2 large onions	*2 tbsp walnut oil*
55 g/2 oz walnuts, crushed	*seasoning*

Wipe the mushrooms clean, but don't bother to peel them.
Discard any stalks that look tough. Slice the mushrooms across
and place them in a large bowl. Peel and thinly slice the onions.
Add them to the mushrooms with the crushed walnuts. Toss well.
Mix the rest of the ingredients together and pour over the salad.
Leave to marinate for 1 hour before serving.

Beetroot salad   Ⓥ

Serves 6
Per serving: 130 kcal/4 g protein/5 g fat/19 g carbohydrate/
5 g fibre

910 g/2 lb raw beetroot	*2 tbsp olive oil*
2 large onions	*1 tsp umbushi vinegar*
2 cloves garlic, crushed	*seasoning*
zest and juice of 1 lemon	

Peel the beetroot and grate it into a large bowl. Peel the onions
and grate them into the bowl. Toss well and add the crushed garlic
with the zest and juice of the lemon. Mix the olive oil, umbushi
vinegar and seasoning together and pour over the salad. Mix
well.

Note: Umbushi vinegar is Japanese, made from salted dried
plums and has a delicious flavour, unlike any other. It can be
bought at health food, Japanese or Chinese stores. If you cannot
find it, you could substitute tarragon vinegar, although this would
make the salad quite different.

Celery and artichoke salad   Ⓥ

Serves 6
Per serving: 125 kcal/3 g protein/5 g fat/18 g carbohydrate/
4 g fibre

12 baby globe artichokes	*zest and juice of 1 lemon*
450 g/1 lb new potatoes	*2 tbsp olive oil*
2 celery hearts	*seasoning*
2 cloves garlic, crushed	

Take all the outside leaves from the artichokes and discard. Boil the central parts for about 15 minutes or until they are tender. Drain well, retaining cooking water. Boil the potatoes in the artichoke water for 20 minutes or until they are just tender. Drain well. Quarter both the artichokes and the potatoes and mix them together in a large bowl. Chop the 2 celery hearts finely and add to the salad. Mix the rest of the ingredients together and pour over the salad.

Celeriac salad $\boxed{V}$

Serves 4
Per serving: 105 kcal/3 g protein/7 g fat/8 g carbohydrate/ 4 g fibre

1 large celeriac root   *1 tbsp white wine vinegar*
2 large onions   *seasoning*
2 cloves garlic, crushed   *handful parsley, chopped*
2 tbsp olive oil

Peel the celeriac root and grate it into a large bowl. Blanch by pouring boiling water over it and leaving for 1 minute. Drain carefully. Peel and grate the onions. Add the onions, crushed garlic, olive oil, wine vinegar and seasoning to the celeriac and toss well. Serve with a little chopped parsley spinkled over the top.

Potato and celeriac

Serves 4
Per serving: 280 kcal/8 g protein/8 g fat/47 g carbohydrate/ 11 g fibre

910 g/2 lb new potatoes   *2 tbsp olive oil*
1 large celeriac root   *zest and juice of 1 lemon*
1 bunch spring onions   *145 ml/5 fl oz low fat yogurt*
2 tbsp capers   *seasoning*

Boil the potatoes in their skins until they are just tender and leave to cool. Peel the celeriac root and dice it into 2.5 cm/1 in chunks. Steam the celeriac chunks for 10-15 minutes so that they are still *al dente*. Allow to cool. Cut the potatoes into quarters and mix them with the celeriac in a large bowl. Chop the spring onions coarsely and add these with the capers. Mix the oil, lemon zest and juice with the yogurt. Season well and pour over the vegetables. Toss thoroughly and serve.

Green bean salad   Ⓥ

Serves 6
Per serving: 190 kcal/10 g protein/12 g fat/12 g carbohydrate/
6 g fibre

225 g/8 oz dried flageolet beans   *zest and juice of 1 lemon*
seasoning   *450 g/1 lb French beans*
2 tbsp olive oil   *450 g/1 lb young broad beans*
2 cloves garlic, crushed   *generous handful fresh mint*

Soak the flageolet beans for a couple of hours then boil them until
tender – about 45 minutes. Drain well. Place the flageolet beans in
a large bowl and season before covering with the olive oil, crushed
garlic, zest and juice of the lemon. Now trim the French beans and
cut into 1.5 cm/½ in chunks. Pod the broad beans. Boil the French
and broad beans in a little water for 5 minutes. Drain and add to
the flageolet beans. Mix thoroughly. Chop the mint very finely
and stir into the salad before serving.

Tuscan bean salad   Ⓥ

Serves 6
Per serving: 260 kcal/17 g protein/7 g fat/34 g carbohydrate/
21 g fibre

115 g/4 oz each: *1 bunch fresh mint, chopped*
  dried haricot beans   *1 bunch fresh chives, chopped*
  dried red kidney beans   *1 bunch fennel leaves, chopped*
  dried black beans   *1 tbsp red wine vinegar*
1 tbsp dried oregano   *2 tbsp olive oil*
450 g/1 lb runner beans   *3 cloves garlic, crushed*
450 g/1 lb broad beans   *seasoning*

Mix the dried beans together and soak them overnight. Drain.
Place the dried beans and oregano in a saucepan, pour plenty of
water over them, bring to the boil for 10 minutes, then simmer for
1½ hours, or until they are tender. Leave to cool.
    Trim the runner beans and cut them into chunks. Pod the broad
beans. Boil or steam the French and broad beans briefly so that
they are just cooked. Drain the dried beans with care and pour
into a large bowl. Drain the fresh beans equally carefully and mix
them with the dried beans. Add the finely chopped herbs and then
the rest of the ingredients. Stir well and leave the salad to marinate
for 1 hour before serving.

Rice and vegetable salad   [V]

Serves 6
Per serving: 120 kcal/3 g protein/5 g fat/16 g carbohydrate/
4 g fibre

1 bunch spring onions
2 green peppers
2 small turnips
2 small carrots
1 small cauliflower
225 g/8 oz cooked brown or white
  long-grain rice

2 cloves garlic, crushed
zest and juice of 1 lemon
2 tbsp olive oil
1 tbsp red wine vinegar
seasoning

Chop the spring onions coarsely. Core and deseed the green peppers and slice them thinly. Grate the turnips and carrots. Slice the cauliflower thinly, crumbling the florets. Place the vegetables and rice in a large bowl and mix thoroughly, making sure that every grain of rice is separate. Add the crushed cloves of garlic and the lemon zest and juice. Then add the oil, vinegar and seasoning. Mix again. Leave for 15 minutes before serving.

Winter salad   [V]

Serves 6
Per serving: 135 kcal/5 g protein/5 g fat/18 g carbohydrate/
9 g fibre

1 white cabbage
4 large carrots
2 large cooking apples
1 large onion
1 fennel root
2 green peppers

zest and juice of 1 lemon
2 cloves garlic, crushed
1 tsp strong mustard
2 tbsp olive oil
seasoning

Trim and grate the cabbage, carrots, cooking apples, onion and fennel root into a large salad bowl. Core and deseed the green peppers and slice them thinly. Add the peppers to the salad with the zest from the lemon. Mix the lemon juice, crushed garlic, mustard, olive oil and seasoning together and pour over the salad. Toss well and leave to rest for 10 minutes before serving.

SAVOURY PASTRIES AND BREADS

In this chapter I take a look at various forms of savoury pastries, as well as giving three examples of different breads. There are recipes for tarts, pies and quiches. All of these names have been blurred by misuse and today, especially in vegetarian cooking, can mean anything. Even traditionally the name pie doesn't necessarily imply pastry – neither cottage pie nor shepherds' pie contain pastry, for example – but here I have defined it in the old English sense of food cooked in a sauce encased completely by pastry, which both keeps in and soaks up the flavour The vegetarian Lenten pies of the Mediterranean countries are famous. A tart can be defined as not containing eggs, but using cream or cheese to thicken it, as in the French classic dish, *Tarte à l'oignon*. A quiche uses cream, eggs and cheese. However, these definitions are no longer used precisely and to avoid overusing saturated fats I have kept these ingredients to a minimum while retaining the true character of the recipes.

For the pastry I have kept to the use of wholemeal flour but if the fats are not mixed well into the flour it can be heavy. Perhaps a mixture of half plain and half wholemeal flour would suit some palates better. This is very much a personal choice, for in a vegetarian diet you are getting enough dietary fibre for you not to have to eat wholemeal flour in every dish; though for flavour it is always best.

I have given a recipe for a high protein loaf which is packed with goodness and two recipes for more unusual breads, one of which uses plain flour.

Cauliflower and fennel pie (V)

Serves 6
Per serving: 365 kcal/9 g protein/23 g fat/33 g carbohydrate/ 8 g fibre

wholemeal pastry made from 225 g/
  8 oz flour (see page 64)
1 small cauliflower

2 heads fennel
1 large onion
25 g/1 oz butter

25 g/1 oz plain flour
285 ml/½ pint vegetable stock
2 tbsp soya sauce

1 tbsp French mustard
freshly ground black pepper

Preheat the oven to 200°C/400°F/gas 6.
Line a greased pie dish 7.5 cm/3 in deep with two-thirds of the pastry. Cut the cauliflower into florets. Trim and quarter the fennel heads. Cut the onion into chunks. Boil all the vegetables in a little water for 5 minutes, so that they are tender but still *al dente*. Arrange them in the pie dish so that they are tightly packed.
Melt the butter in a pan, add the flour and make a roux. Add the vegetable stock slowly with the soya sauce and the mustard to make a sauce. Add the pepper and taste for seasoning. Pour the sauce over the vegetables in the pie. Roll out the remaining third of the pastry to make the lid. Cover the pie, pressing the edges together firmly.
Bake in the oven for 40 minute, protecting the top of the pie with buttered paper for the first 30 minutes. If the inside is not steaming after 40 minutes, cook for a further 10 minutes.

Swiss chard pie

Serves 6

See photograph, page 67

Per serving: 500 kcal/21 g protein/33 g fat/32 g carbohydrate/ 9 g fibre

wholemeal pastry made from 225 g/
*   8 oz flour (see page 64)*
450 g/1 lb Swiss chard
pinch grated nutmeg
25 g/1 oz butter or margarine
25 g/1 oz plain flour

285 ml/½ pint semi-skimmed milk
55 g/2 oz Gruyère, grated
55 g/2 oz Parmesan, grated
seasoning
4 eggs, hard-boiled

Preheat the oven to 175°C/350°F/gas 4.
Use two-thirds of the pastry to line a greased pie dish 7.5 cm/3 in deep. Chop the Swiss chard coarsely and cook in its own juice in a closed saucepan for about 12 minutes. Let it cool, then add the nutmeg and liquidize to a coarse purée.
Melt the butter in a saucepan and add the flour to make a roux. Add the milk and cheese to make a thick sauce. Check seasoning. Pour the sauce over the Swiss chard and mix thoroughly. Pour the mixture into the pie dish. Slice the hard-boiled eggs in half and push down into the chard. Roll out the remaining pastry to make a lid. Cover the pie with the pastry lid, pushing all the edges together firmly. Protect the top of the pie with buttered paper. Place the pie in the oven and bake for 50 minutes. Remove the buttered paper from the top for the last 12 minutes of cooking.

Aubergine and bean pie (V)

Serves 6
Per serving: 415 kcal/11 g protein/25 g fat/39 g carbohydrate/
11 g fibre

85 g/3 oz dried red kidney beans
1 large aubergine
2 tbsp olive oil
675 g/1 lb 8 oz tomatoes
3 tbsp tomato purée

2 tbsp soya sauce
handful basil, finely chopped
seasoning
wholemeal pastry made from 225 g/
8 oz flour (see page 64)

Preheat the oven 175°C/350°F/gas 4.

Having soaked the beans overnight, boil them fiercely for 10 minutes. Throw away the water and start cooking again. Simmer the beans in plenty of water for 1½ hours or until they are tender. Drain carefully and reserve.

Slice the aubergine into 0.75 cm/¼ in pieces. Sprinkle salt on them and leave for 1 hour to get rid of the bitter juices. Rinse the aubergine thoroughly under the cold tap and pat dry. Heat the olive oil in the pan and fry the aubergine briefly on both sides.

Peel the tomatoes by blanching them in boiling water, then cook them over a low heat in a closed saucepan for about 5 minutes. Add the tomato purée, soya sauce and basil. Check flavour and season if necessary.

Mix the aubergine, beans and tomato sauce together. Line a greased pie dish 7.5 cm/3 in deep with two-thirds of the pastry and fill the dish with the vegetable mixture. Roll out the remaining pastry for the top and fit the lid on the pie. Protect the top with buttered paper and bake the pie in the oven for 50 minutes. Remove the buttered paper for the last 12 minutes of cooking.

Courgette tart

Serves 6
Per serving: 245 kcal/8 g protein/16 g fat/18 g carbohydrate/
4 g fibre

For 20–22.5 cm/8–9 in pastry
  case:
115 g/4 oz wholemeal flour
½ tsp baking powder
½ tsp salt
55 g/2 oz butter
2 tsp corn oil
2–3 tbsp water

For the filling:
450 g/1 lb courgettes
25 g/1 oz butter
1 small onion, chopped
1 tbsp chopped fresh tarragon
1 tbsp chopped fresh parsley
2 eggs
145 ml/5 fl oz low fat yogurt
25 g/1 oz Parmesan, grated
seasoning

First, make the pastry case. Mix the flour with the baking powder and salt. Take the butter straight from the refrigerator and grate it into the flour. Rub the fat and flour together until the mixture resembles small breadcrumbs. Add the oil and water slowly until you have made a stiff paste. Wrap the paste in cling film or foil and refrigerate for 1 hour.

Preheat the oven to 200°C/400°F/gas 6. Remove the pastry from the refrigerator and leave to return to room temperature, then roll it out to fit the tart tin. Prick the base and fill with dried beans before baking blind in the oven for 5–8 minutes. Take the pastry case out of the oven and remove the beans. Set aside to await the filling.

Preheat the oven to 180°C/350°F/gas 4.

Cut the unpeeled courgettes into dice. Melt the butter in a pan and add the diced courgettes, chopped onion and herbs. Cook over a moderate heat for about 5 minutes. Allow to cool before beating in the eggs, yogurt and grated Parmesan. Season. Pour the mixture into the pastry case and bake in the oven for about 40 minutes. Serve hot or cold.

Mushroom tart

Serves 6
Per serving: 245 kcal/8 g protein/16 g fat/18 g carbohydrate/ 4 g fibre

450 g/1 lb mushrooms	*bunch spring onions, chopped*
225 g/8 oz onions	*285 ml/½ pt low fat yogurt*
25 g/1 oz butter	*seasoning*
25 g/1 oz Parmesan, grated	*20–20.5/8–9 in wholemeal pastry*
25 g/1 oz Gruyère, grated	*case, baked blind (see page 64)*

Preheat the oven to 218°C/425°F/gas 7.

Slice the mushrooms and the onions. Melt the butter in a saucepan and cook the sliced vegetables over a low heat for 5 minutes. Leave to cool then add the Parmesan, Gruyère, spring onions and yogurt. Stir thoroughly and season. Spoon the mixture into the prepared pastry case and bake in the oven for 30 minutes.

Onion tart

Serves 6   See photograph, page 67
Per serving: 200 kcal/6 g protein/12 g fat/18 g carbohydrate/ 3 g fibre

450 g/1 lb onions	*1 egg*
12 g/½ oz butter or margarine	*145 ml/5 fl oz skimmed milk*

2 tbsp green peppercorns
pinch grated nutmeg
seasoning

20–22.5 cm/8–9 in wholemeal pastry
case, baked blind (see page 64)
12 black olives, stoned

Preheat the oven to 175°C/350°F/gas 4.
Chop the onions. Melt the butter in a pan and cook the onions until they are soft – about 10 minutes. Beat the egg into the milk and then mix into the pan with the onions. Add the peppercorns, nutmeg and seasoning. Mix thoroughly. Pour into the pastry case and arrange the olives in a pattern on the tart. Place in the oven and bake for about 40 minutes.

Pepper and leek tart

Serves 6
Per serving: 270 kcal/7 g protein/ 18 g fat/21 g carbohydrate/ 5 g fibre

3 green peppers
450 g/1 lb leeks
55 g/2 oz butter
1 egg
285 ml/½ pint skimmed milk

3 tbsp parsley, chopped
seasoning
20–22.5 cm/8–9 in wholemeal pastry
case, baked blind (see page 64)

Preheat the oven to 175°C/350°F/gas 4.
Core and deseed the peppers. Chop them coarsely. Wash the leeks thoroughly and chop them. Melt the butter and cook both the peppers and leeks in a covered pan for about 15 minutes. Beat the egg into the milk and add to the peppers and leeks, mixing thoroughly. Add the parsley and seasoning and mix again. Pour into the prepared pastry case. Bake in the oven for about 40 minutes.

Tomato and oatmeal tart

Serves 6
Per serving: 320 kcal/11 g protein/18 g fat/30 g carbohydrate/ 5 g fibre

For the base:
115 g/4 oz rolled oats
115 g/4 oz wholemeal flour
½ tsp salt
85 g/3 oz butter or hard margarine
1 large egg, beaten

For the filling:
675 g/1 lb 8 oz tomatoes
4 cloves garlic, crushed
1 small chilli, deseeded and chopped
25 g/1 oz Parmesan, grated
25 g/1 oz Gruyère, grated
1 egg
seasoning

Swiss chard pie (*above*, see page 63), Onion tart (*below*, see page 65).

Preheat the oven to 175°C/350°F/gas 4.

Mix the oats and flour together with the salt. Rub in the fat and add the egg to make a paste. Refrigerate for an hour. Allow the dough to return to room temperature then roll it out. Line a 20–22.5 cm/8–9 in tart tin, cover with dried beans and bake blind.

Cook the tomatoes with the garlic and chilli in a saucepan over a low heat then put them through a sieve and throw away the skins. Add the cheeses to the tomato purée and beat in the egg. Season and pour into the pastry case. Place the tart on a baking sheet and bake for 30–35 minutes.

Spinach quiche

Serves 6
Per serving: 350 kcal/21 g protein/24 g fat/14 g carbohydrate/ 8 g fibre

450 g/1 lb leaf spinach
115 g/4 oz low fat quark
115 g/4 oz double Gloucester cheese, grated
55 g/2 oz Parmesan, grated
pinch nutmeg

seasoning
4 eggs
wholemeal pastry case to line 20–22.5 cm/8–9 in quiche dish, baked blind (see page 64)

Preheat the oven to 200°C/400°F/gas 6.

Cook the spinach in its own juice until its bulk has reduced by two-thirds. Remove from the heat and allow to cool. Next, add the quark, double Gloucester cheese and the Parmesan. Add the nutmeg and seasoning. Beat the eggs into the mixture and gently pour it into the pastry case. Bake in the oven for 30 minutes.

Roquefort quiche

Serves 6
Per serving: 315 kcal/14 g protein/23 g fat/14 g carbohydrate/ 2 g fibre

1 bunch parsley
1 bunch spring onions
170 g/6 oz Roquefort, crumbled
85 g/3 oz low fat quark
85 g/3 oz cottage cheese
3 tbsp low fat yogurt

2 egg whites
1 egg
seasoning
wholemeal pastry case to line 20–22.5 cm/8–9 in quiche dish, baked blind (see page 64)

Corn bread (*above*, see page 71), Roquefort quiche (*below*)

Preheat the oven to 190°C/375°F/gas 5.

Chop the parsley and onions. Mix the Roquefort, quark, cottage cheese and yogurt. Add to the parsley and onions. Beat the egg whites and 1 egg into the mixture. Season. Smooth the mixture into the prepared pastry case and place in the oven. Bake for 30–40 minutes.

Quiche au ratatouille

Serves 6
Per serving: 350 kcal/10 g protein/26 g fat/21 g carbohydrate/ 6 g fibre

1 aubergine	*seasoning*
2 green peppers	*handful fresh parsley, chopped*
2 courgettes	*3 eggs*
2 onions	*55 g/2 oz mature Cheddar, grated*
4 tbsp olive oil	*wholemeal pastry case to line a*
5 cloves garlic, crushed	*20–22.5 cm/8–9 in quiche dish,*
450 g/1 lb tomatoes, peeled	*baked blind (see page 64)*

Preheat the oven to 218°C/425°F/gas 7.

Slice the aubergine into 0.75 cm/¼ in pieces and sprinkle them with salt. Leave for 1 hour then rinse well under the cold tap. Pat dry. Core and deseed the peppers. Chop the courgettes and onions. Pour the oil into a frying pan and place all the vegetables in it to cook, adding the crushed garlic. Cook gently for 15 minutes before adding the peeled tomatoes. Continue to cook for another 10 minutes. Season and stir in the fresh parsley. Remove from heat.

When the vegetables are cool beat in the eggs and the grated cheese. Pour the mixture into the pastry case and bake for 30 minutes.

High protein loaf

Makes 3 loaves
Total recipe: 4890 kcal/204 g protein/120 g fat/803 g carbohydrate/116 g fibre

Per slice (12 slices per loaf): 135 kcal/6 g protein/3 g fat/ 22 g carbohydrate/3 g fibre

825 ml–1.15 1/1½–2 pt water	*3 tbsp soya flour*
15 g/½ oz dried yeast or 25 g/1 oz	*3 tbsp bran*
fresh yeast	*4 tbsp wheat germ*
1 kg/2¼ lb wholemeal flour	*3 tbsp linseeds*
1 tsp sea salt	*3 tbsp seasame seeds*
3 tbsp crushed wheat	*1 tbsp dried brewers' yeast*

4 tbsp skimmed milk powder *2 tbsp treacle*
3 tbsp olive oil *1 tbsp malt extract*

This recipe needs no kneading. The trick is to add enough water to get the dough tacky but not too much, so that the end product will be moist and fairly light. The point about the recipe is that most of the additions are high protein ingredients which will flavour the loaf. It is excellent toasted and makes a good start to the day.

Preheat the oven to 275°C/450°F/gas 8.

Choose a very large bowl for mixing. Warm a few tablespoons of the water and pour over the yeast in the bowl. Leave the yeast to work, and when it has begun to froth and bubble, add the rest of the dry ingredients. Mix thoroughly and continue to mix while gradually adding enough of the warmed water. Too little and the loaf will be hard, too much and it will sink in the middle. It is a matter of trial and error. The dough must be elastic throughout, which means that the yeast has permeated through the mixture, so continue to stir until it feels right.

Oil 3 × 500 g/1 lb loaf tins and pour the mixture in. Put the tins in plastic bags in a warm place and leave to rise until doubled in size. Once risen, bake the loaves in the oven for 15 minutes, then lower the heat to 175°C/350°F/gas 4 and cook for a further 20 minutes. When the loaves are done, turn out immediately on to wire cooling racks.

Corn bread

Makes 3 loaves See photograph, page 68

Total recipe: 2330 kcal/115 g protein/111 g fat/233 g carbohydrate/17 g fibre

Per slice (12 slices per loaf): 65 kcal/3 g protein/3 g fat/6 g carbohydrate/1 g fibre

25 g/1 oz butter *285 ml/½ pt semi-skimmed milk*
2 onions, chopped *115 g/4 oz Gruyère, grated*
4 sweetcorn cobs *225 g/8 oz cottage cheese*
200 g/7 oz cornmeal *6 eggs*
1 tsp sea salt *1 tsp dried aniseed*

Preheat the oven to 200°C/400°F/gas 6.

Melt the butter in a pan and cook the chopped onions until they are soft. Boil the sweetcorn cobs for 15 minutes and strip off the kernels with a sharp knife. Mix together the cornmeal, kernels, salt and milk. Add the onions, Gruyére and cottage cheese. Mix with an electric mixer if possible so that everything is well blended. Separate the eggs and add the yolks to the mixture with the aniseed, beating well. Beat the egg whites until they are stiff and fold them into the mixture. Oil 3 × 500 g/1 lb loaf tins, pour in the mixture and bake for 45 minutes. Cool on a wire rack.

Fruit loaf (V)

Total recipe: 1570 kcal/44 g protein/10 g fat/347 g carbohydrate/
38 g fibre

Per slice (12 slices per loaf): 130 kcal/4 g protein/1 g fat/
29 g carbohydrate/3 g fibre

225 g/8 oz strong plain flour	*1 tsp ground mixed spice*
1½ tsp baking powder	*285 ml/½ pt semi-skimmed milk or*
1 tsp salt	*unsweetened soya milk*
115 g/4 oz sultanas	*2 tbsp malt extract*
55 g/2 oz chopped dates	*1 tbsp black treacle*
55 g/2 oz currants	*1 tbsp honey*
1 tsp grated nutmeg	

Preheat oven to 150°C/325°F/gas 3.

Sieve the flour, baking powder and salt together into a basin. Add all the dried fruit and the spice. Pour the milk into a saucepan and add the malt extract, treacle and honey. Stir over a low heat until it is lukewarm and well mixed. Pour into the flour and dried fruit, mixing well with a wooden spoon. Beat the mixture to a soft dough. Grease a 500 g/1 lb loaf tin and press the dough into the tin. Bake for 1 hour. Remove from the oven and cool on a wire rack.

BEAN AND GRAIN DISHES

These dishes are considered to be the staple vegetarian food, and to some degree have done harm to the idea of the cuisine being considered a gourmet one, because they have bequeathed the stigma of stodge and blandness. Indeed, there is a lot of truth in this. You cannot cook light, airy meals with a lot of beans and grains; but you can use a little of each to complement other dishes. It is all a matter of balance and harmony – which is what the art of cooking is about as much as any other art.

The pulse family needs flavourings to lift their earthiness. Use plenty of fresh herbs and when these are not available, dried herbs and spices. Use also flavoured oils like walnut and sesame to start the cooking, or add a tablespoon at the end. Even the flavoured vinegars can help. But one of the best additions in the cooking of pulses is the rind of lemon, orange or tamarind. One of these with bay leaves or a sprig of rosemary is a great help.

Baked beans ☑

Serves 4
Per serving: 180 kcal/10 g protein/5 g fat/25 g carbohydrate/
5 g fibre

170 g/6 oz dried haricot beans
400 g /14 oz can tomatoes
3 tbsp tomato purée
1 tbsp brown sugar

55 g/2 oz vegan margarine, eg,
  Mapleton's Nutter
seasoning

Preheat the oven to 150°C/325°F/gas 3.
  Having soaked the beans overnight, boil them fiercely for 10 minutes before throwing away the water. Pour the beans into a large ovenproof pot. Add the canned tomatoes, tomato purée, brown sugar and Nutter. Add enough water to cover the top of the beans by 4 cm/1½ in. Place a tightly fitting lid on the pot and place in the oven. Cook for 3–4 hours. Taste and season when the beans are tender.

Caribbean black beans ☑

Serves 4
Per serving: 225 kcal/12 g protein/9 g fat/26 g carbohydrate/
14 g fibre

225 g/8 oz dried black beans
2 tbsp olive oil
1 tsp oregano
1 tsp sage

2 dried red chillis
55 g/2 oz ginger root, grated
seasoning

Soak the beans overnight then boil them fiercely for 10 minutes before throwing away the water. Heat the oil in a large saucepan and add the herbs, grated ginger and chillis. Throw the black beans in and stir well, cooking the mixture in the oil for a few moments. Add enough water to cover the beans by 4 cm/1½ in. Leave to simmer for 2 hours or until tender. Drain the beans well, remove the chillis and season before serving.

Mexican beans ☑

Serves 4
Per serving: 260 kcal/14 g protein/9 g fat/32 g carbohydrate/
17 g fibre

225 g/8 oz dried red kidney beans
2 tbsp olive oil
1 tsp oregano
3 cloves garlic, crushed

2 dried red chillis
400 g/14 oz can tomatoes
2 red peppers
1 large onion

Soak the beans overnight then boil fiercely for 10 minutes before throwing away the water. Heat half the oil in a saucepan and add the oregano, garlic and dried chillis. Add the beans and cook for a moment or two before adding the canned tomatoes and enough water to cover the beans by 4 cm/1½ in. Simmer the mixture for 1½ hours or until the beans are tender.

Once the beans are cooked, core and deseed the red peppers. Chop them and cook in the rest of the oil. Slice the onion into very thin rings. When the peppers are tender – about 5 minutes – drain the beans of any excess water and add the red peppers in their oil. Stir in the raw onion rings. Remove the chillis, put the lid back on the pan and allow the beans to rest, away from the heat, for 10 minutes before serving.

Green bean stew

Serves 4   See photograph, page 78
Per serving: 200 kcal/11 g protein/8 g fat/23 g carbohydrate/ 4 g fibre

170 g/6 oz dried flageolet beans
1.15 1/2 pt celery stock (see page 46)
2 bay leaves
225 g/8 oz French beans
450 g/1 lb broad beans, podded

145 ml/5 fl oz pesto sauce (available from Italian delicatessens)
25 g/1 oz butter
25 g/1 oz plain flour
285 ml/½ pt semi-skimmed milk
seasoning

Soak the flageolet beans for 2 hours then drain and simmer them in the celery stock with the bay leaves for 1 hour. Meanwhile, trim and slice the French beans and cook them with the podded broad beans in a little water until just tender. Drain and add to the cooked flageolet beans, removing the bay leaves. Mix in the pesto sauce.

Melt the butter in a pan, add the flour and make a roux. Slowly add the milk to make a sauce. Season and add the sauce to the beans. Stir well and return to the heat briefly to warm through before serving.

Fasoulia   V

Serves 4
Per serving: 270 kcal/13 g protein/12 g fat/30 g carbohydrate/ 15 g fibre

225 g/8 oz dried haricot beans
3 tbsp olive oil
10 cloves garlic, crushed
½ tsp thyme
½ tsp sage

2 tsp oregano
2 bay leaves
2 tbsp tomato purée
1 large onion, finely sliced into rings
seasoning

Soak the beans overnight then boil fiercely for 10 minutes before throwing away the water. Heat the olive oil in a large heavy saucepan and throw in the drained beans with the garlic and herbs. Toss in the oil for a moment then add enough boiling water to cover the beans by 2.5 cm/1 in. Stir in the tomato purée. Cover the pan and cook over a very low heat for 3 hours.

Once the beans are tender, add the sliced onion rings and seasoning and replace the lid. Leave away from the heat for 10 minutes. Best eaten warm or cold.

Chick pea and spinach casserole (V)

Serves 4
Per serving: 400 kcal/17 g protein/16 g fat/50 g carbohydrate/ 16 g fibre

170 g/6 oz dried chick peas *3 cloves garlic, crushed*
450 g/1 lb potatoes *285 ml/½ pt dry cider*
25 g/1 oz butter or margarine *3 tbsp mint, finely chopped*
2 tbsp olive oil *seasoning*
450 g/1 lb leaf spinach, chopped

Soak the chick peas overnight and cook them in boiling water for 2 hours. Drain well. Cut the potatoes into quarters and cook in lightly salted water until they are tender. Add the potatoes to the chick peas. Melt the butter and olive oil in a pan and add the chopped spinach and crushed garlic. Cook over a low heat for 10 minutes. Add the cider to the chick peas and potatoes and boil fiercely for 2 minutes. Now add the spinach and its juice, stirring well. Finally, add the chopped mint and seasoning. Reheat before serving.

Green lentil dhal Ⅴ

Serves 4
Per serving: 240 kcal/14 g protein/8 g fat/30 g carbohydrate/ 7 g fibre

225 g/8 oz green lentils *1 tsp coriander*
2 tbsp sunflower oil *1½ tsp turmeric*
55 g/2 oz ginger root, grated *1 tbsp garam masala*
3 cloves garlic, crushed *seasoning*
1 tsp ground cumin

Soak the green lentils for ½ hour. Heat the oil in a pan and add the grated ginger root, garlic and spices. Cook these for a moment before adding the drained lentils. Pour boiling water into the pan to cover the lentils by about 2.5 cm/1 in. Cook over a low heat for about 30 minutes, stirring occasionally so that the lentils do not stick.

If a smooth purée is desired, the lentils may now be blended, but I prefer them as they are. Season and turn out into an ovenproof dish and keep the dahl warm until ready to serve.

Khichhari   ⟦V⟧

Serves 4
Per serving: 520 kcal/18 g protein/19 g fat/75 g carbohydrate/ 10 g fibre

115 g/4 oz brown lentils	*cumin*
115 g/4 oz dried green split peas	*coriander*
60 ml/2 fl oz sunflower oil	*mustard seed*
2 onions, sliced	*1 tbsp raisins*
55 g/2 oz ginger root, grated	*1 tbsp almonds*
½ tsp each:	*1 tbsp cashew nuts*
crushed cinnamon bark	*170 g/6 oz long-grain rice*
cardamom	*1.15l/2 pt boiling water*
nutmeg	*seasoning*
mace	

Preheat the oven to 175°C/350°F/gas 4.

Soak the lentils and split green peas for 30 minutes. Drain well. Heat the oil in a large pan and fry the onions, ginger and all the spices for a few minutes. Add the raisins and nuts and let them brown a little. Add the rice, lentils and split peas and mix thoroughly. Pour in the boiling water, mix and pour the mixture into an ovenproof dish with a tightly fitting lid. Bake in the oven for 30–40 minutes. Season well before serving.

Kosheri   (V)

Serves 4
Per serving: 470 kcal/19 g protein/6 g fat/90 g carbohydrate/ 12 g fibre

170 g/6 oz long-grain rice	For the hot sauce:
115 g/4 oz green lentils	*1 tsp ground cumin*
115 g/4 oz wholemeal macaroni	*1 tsp ground coriander*
seasoning	*½ tsp chilli powder*
910 g/2 lb tomatoes	*½ tsp celery salt*
2 onions	*4 tbsp tomato purée*
145 ml/5 fl oz semi-skimmed milk or	*200 ml/7 fl oz vegetable stock (see*
unsweetened soya milk	*page 46)*
55 g/2 oz plain flour	
60 ml/2 fl oz sunflower oil	

Kosheri

OVERLEAF: Green bean stew (*left*, see page 74), Indian rice (*centre*, see page 92), Buckwheat noodles with mushroom sauce (*right*, see page 85)

Cook the rice, lentils and macaroni separately, drain well and season each to taste. Set aside.

Put the tomatoes in a saucepan and cook over a moderate heat until they have become a pulp. Put them through a sieve and season the resulting tomato sauce.

Slice the onions into rings and let them soak in the milk for a few moments. Place the flour in a paper bag and put the drained onions in the bag. Shake so that the onions are evenly covered in flour. Pour the oil into a frying pan and fry the onions until they are crisp. Drain on absorbent paper and set aside.

Make the hot sauce by mixing the spices and tomato purée together in a bowl. Pour the heated vegetable stock over the mixture in the bowl and stir to make a paste.

To assemble the kosheri: tip out the rice on to a large serving platter so that it covers the whole surface. Now tip out the lentils in the centre of the rice. Now tip out the macaroni into the centre of the lentils. Drizzle the tomato sauce over each layer, garnish with the crisply fried onions and serve the kosheri with the hot sauce on the table.

Millet and bean croquettes

Serves 4
Per serving: 270 kcal/12 g protein/10 g fat/35 g carbohydrate/
9 g fibre

115 g/4 oz dried split mung beans
2 tbsp olive oil
115 g/4 oz millet
2 onions, finely chopped
1 tsp dried oregano
2 tsp dried sage
3 cloves garlic, crushed

2 tbsp shoyu sauce (available from
  Chinese stores)
1 egg, beaten
1 tbsp gram flour
handful fresh parsley, chopped
seasoning

Soak the mung beans for 2 hours, then bring them to the boil and simmer for 20 minutes. In another pan use a little of the oil to cook the millet for a few minutes until it just turns brown. Pour boiling water over the millet and simmer for 20 minutes. Take from the heat and leave to stand. Meanwhile, with the rest of the oil, cook the chopped onions with the oregano, sage and garlic until soft.

Drain the mung beans well and mash to a rough purée. Squeeze all the moisture from the millet and add to the beans. Mix in the onions and herbs. Add the shoyu sauce and the beaten egg and then the parsley and seasoning. Mix thoroughly and mix in the gram flour to bind. Pour a little oil into a frying pan and, when it is really hot, drop tablespoons of the mixture into the hot oil and

Millet and bean croquettes (*above*), Polenta (*below*, see page 83)

cook until each side is brown and crisp. Do not overcrowd the pan. Drain the croquettes on absorbent paper and keep warm until you are ready to serve.

Millet pilav

Serves 4
Per serving: 370 kcal/13 g protein/16 g fat/46 g carbohydrate/ 4 g fibre

2 red peppers	570 ml/1 pt vegetable stock (see
1 onion	page 46)
2 courgettes	45 g/1½ oz Parmesan, grated
2 tbsp olive oil	45 g/1½ oz Gruyère, grated
3 cloves garlic, crushed	handful fresh parsley, finely chopped
225 g/8 oz millet	seasoning

Core and deseed the red peppers. Chop them with the onion and courgettes. Heat the oil in a pan and cook the chopped vegetables with the crushed garlic for a few moments. Add the millet, stirring the grains into the oil, and cook until the millet goes brown. Add the stock and simmer over a very low heat in a tightly covered saucepan for 20 minutes. Stir in the grated cheeses and the parsely. Season before serving.

Hot tabouleh   Ⅴ

Serves 4
Per serving: 260 kcal/5 g protein/13 g fat/33 g carbohydrate/ 4 g fibre

3 tbsp olive oil	1 bunch parsley, finely chopped
170 g/6 oz buckwheat (unroasted)	1 bunch spring onions, chopped
5 cloves garlic, crushed	seasoning
zest and juice of 2 lemons	
835 ml/1½ pt vegetable stock (see	
page 46)	

Heat the oil in a large saucepan and add the buckwheat with the crushed garlic. Stir well and allow to cook for a moment or two. Add the lemon zest and juice, pour on the stock, bring to the boil and simmer for 10 minutes. Let the mixture stand in a covered saucepan for a further 10 minutes. If any liquid remains, drain it away, then add the parsley and spring onions. Season well before serving.

Tabouleh can be used as a delicious alternative for rice.

Note: Buckwheat is also sold as bulgar wheat or cracked wheat.

Buckwheat rissoles

Serves 4
Per serving: 240 kcal/7 g protein/10 g fat/33 g carbohydrate/
4 g fibre

170 g/6 oz buckwheat (unroasted)	*1 egg, beaten*
3 cloves garlic, crushed	*1 generous handful parsley, chopped*
3 tbsp tomato purée	*1 generous handful chives, chopped*
1 tsp ground cumin	*seasoning*
1 tsp coriander	*2 tbsp sunflower oil*
1 tbsp garam masala	

Pour the buckwheat into a bowl and cover with boiling water.
Leave for 20 minutes then drain thoroughly. Add all the rest of the
ingredients, except the oil, and stir well. Heat the oil. Make small
cakes of the mixture and fry in the hot oil until crisp and
browned.

Polenta

Makes 12 sticks   See photograph, page 80
Per stick: 95 kcal/1 g protein/3 g fat/17 g carbohydrate/1 g fibre

1.15 1/2 pt water	For the coating:
225 g/8 oz cornmeal	*1 egg, beaten*
1 tsp sea salt	*extra cornmeal*
	corn oil for frying

Bring the water to the boil in a large saucepan. Pour the cornmeal
into the water in a slow, steady stream, stirring all the time. Add
the salt and lower the heat. Cover the saucepan and cook for a
further 15 minutes. Have a peep into the pan every so often to
make sure that the polenta hasn't stuck to the sides of the pan or
become lumpy. Lightly grease a shallow dish and pour the polenta
in. Smooth it down so that it is quite level and leave to rest
overnight.

Next day, cut the polenta into small rectangles the size of half a
piece of toast. Dip these into the beaten egg and roll them in the
extra cornmeal so that they are evenly coated. Heat the corn oil in
a pan until it is very hot. Fry the pieces of polenta until they are
brown. Drain well. They can be eaten hot, with a spicy sauce, or in
place of bread to accompany other dishes.

Barley and sweetcorn casserole

Serves 4
Per serving: 290 kcal/6 g protein/9 g fat/50 g carbohydrate/
4 g fibre

2 tbsp olive oil	*4 sweetcorn cobs*
225 g/8 oz pot barley	*145 ml/5 fl oz low fat yogurt*
825 ml/1½ pt vegetable stock (see page	*seasoning*
46)	

Heat the olive oil in a pan. Pour in the barley and fry for a few minutes. Pour on the vegetable stock and bring to the boil. Simmer for about 50 minutes until the barley is cooked. Carefully drain off any remaining liquid. Leave to cool.

Boil the corn on the cob for 10 minutes. Drain. When cool, scrape off the kernels with a sharp knife and add them to the barley. Mix in the yogurt. Stir well, season and serve.

PASTA, RICE AND PIZZA

You can now buy excellent wholemeal pasta in the large stores as well as the smaller delicatessens. The best health food shops have been selling it for years in a variety of shapes and sizes. Gourmets of Italian food shudder at the thought, believing that it will make the traditional dishes too heavy. This is not so – wholemeal pasta gives greater flavour to the dish and it is easier to time the cooking so that the pasta is *al dente*.

Among the best noodles on sale in this country are buckwheat and come from Japan with the trade name Soba. These noodles have plenty of flavour and are very simple to cook. They are blanched in boiling water and left for eight minutes.

Some of the best traditional Italian dishes are the simplest. For many years I have been addicted to the Neapolitan method with spaghetti – *Spaghetti all' aglio*. You can order this dish in any tiny restaurant all over Sicily. It is simply several cloves of garlic chopped up small and sprinkled over the spaghetti with a little olive oil or butter. Washed down with a glass of rough red wine and eaten in the sun, on the quayside, it is a perfect lunch.

I must here confess to a blasphemy – I don't much care for brown rice. It isn't that I dislike the taste, it's obviously superior to white, it's simply that after one mouthful I have lost all appetite. For this reason there are no brown rice recipes in this book. However, for readers who enjoy the virtues of brown rice, the recipes can be adapted, remembering that brown rice needs 45–50 minutes' cooking time.

Italian purists have also complained over the years that risottos must be cooked on top of the oven and not inside. I prefer using the inside of the oven, as then the rice never sticks to the bottom of the pan. It has been said too that my pizza dough bears no resemblance to real pizza dough. I don't apologize. This is the way I like it and it tastes like the real thing to me.

Buckwheat noodles with mushroom sauce

Serves 4   See photograph, page 79
Per serving: 360 kcal/12 g protein/8 g fat/65 g carbohydrate/ 7 g fibre

340 g/12 oz buckwheat noodles (see page 84)
225 g/8 oz mushrooms
25 g/1 oz butter or margarine

seasoning
145 ml/5 fl oz low fat yogurt
1 tbsp shoyu sauce (available from Chinese stores)

Pour boiling water over the noodles. Cover and leave for 8 minutes.

Meanwhile, make the sauce by chopping the mushrooms finely, melting the butter in a pan, and cooking the mushrooms in the butter with the seasoning for 5 minutes. Pour the yogurt and the shoyu sauce into the pan and reheat very gently, stirring well.

Drain the noodles with care. Pour the sauce over the noodles and serve at once.

Fettucine with soft cheese

Serves 4
Per serving: 330 kcal/20 g protein/8 g fat/48 g carbohydrate/ 7 g fibre

285 g/10 oz wholemeal fettucine
115 g/4 oz low fat quark
25 g/1 oz Parmesan, grated

pinch nutmeg
seasoning

Preheat the oven to 175°C/350°F/gas 4.
Cook the pasta in plenty of boiling salted water. Drain well. Butter a shallow ovenproof dish and pour the cooked pasta into it.

Mix all the remaining ingredients together and stir them into the pasta. Place the mixture in the oven for about 5 minutes, until the cheeses have melted.

Tagliatelle with eggs and herbs

Serves 4   See photograph, page 89

Per serving: 360 kcal/15 g protein/10 g fat/56 g carbohydrate/ 9 g fibre

340 g/12 oz wholemeal tagliatelle   *1 bunch basil, finely chopped*
25 g/1 oz butter   *2 eggs, beaten*
1 bunch parsley, finely chopped   *seasoning*

Cook the pasta in plenty of boiling, salted water for 5 minutes. Drain well. Melt the butter in a large shallow pan. Add the herbs, the beaten eggs and seasoning. Before the eggs have set, empty the tagliatelle into the pan and move the mixture round, so that the eggs and herbs cook on to the pasta. Serve immediately.

Macaroni cheese

Serves 4

Per serving: 495 kcal/25 g protein/21 g fat/55 g carbohydrate/ 7 g fibre

285 ml/½ pt skimmed milk   *55 g/2 oz Gruyère, grated*
3 bay leaves   *25 g/1 oz butter*
285 g/10 oz wholemeal macaroni   *25 g/1 oz plain flour*
55 g/2 oz sage Derby cheese, grated   *seasoning*
55 g/2 oz Parmesan, grated   *1 bunch fresh parsley, finely chopped*

Preheat the oven to 200°C/400°F/gas 6.

Heat the milk with the bay leaves in it and then remove from the heat and leave to allow the bay leaves to infuse. Meanwhile, boil the macaroni in plenty of salted water for 5 minutes, or until it is just cooked. Drain well.

Take a deep ovenproof dish and butter it. Lay one-third of the macaroni in the bottom, sprinkle it with the grated sage Derby. Put another third of the pasta into the dish and sprinkle with the Parmesan. Then add the last of the macaroni and sprinkle that with the Gruyère.

Make a roux with the butter and flour. Remove the bay leaves from the milk and pour the milk into the roux, stirring continuously. Check seasoning. Stir in the chopped parsley and pour the sauce over the macaroni. Place in the oven and bake for 25–30 minutes.

Note: If you cannot find sage Derby, use any hard cheese such as Cheddar and add a pinch of sage.

Cannelloni with walnut cheese

Serves 4
Per serving: 390 kcal/22 g protein/25 g fat/21 g carbohydrate/
3 g fibre

12 sheets wholemeal cannelloni	*25 g/1 oz butter*
1 bunch spring onions	*25 g/1 oz flour*
85 g/3 oz broken walnuts	*285 ml/½ pt skimmed milk*
285 ml/½ pt cottage cheese	*25 g/1 oz Gruyère, grated*
55 g/2 oz Parmesan, grated	*seasoning*
55 g/2 oz wholemeal breadcrumbs	

Preheat the oven to 175°C/350°F/gas 4.

Cook the cannelloni in plenty of boiling water for about 10 minutes or until tender. Drain well.

Make the stuffing by chopping the spring onions and mixing them with the walnuts, cottage cheese and Parmesan. Add the breadcrumbs and mix thoroughly. Now make the sauce by melting the butter in a pan and adding the flour to make a roux. Stir in the milk and, finally, add the Gruyère and seasoning.

Place a small piece of cheese stuffing on each sheet of cannelloni. Roll the pasta over, tucking in each end from the top. Place the cannelloni rolls in a buttered baking dish and pour a little of the sauce over each one. Bake in the oven for 15 minutes.

Stuffed pancakes

Makes 8 pancakes
Total recipe: 1550 kcal/64 g protein/101 g fat/103 g carbohydrate/
10 g fibre

For the batter:

115 g/4oz wholemeal flour	
½ tsp salt	*55 g/2 oz Roquefort*
2 eggs	*1 bunch spring onions, chopped*
1 tbsp olive oil	*1 bunch parsley, chopped*
285 ml/½ pt milk and water, mixed	*1 egg*
	seasoning
For the stuffing:	*tomato sauce (see page 76, but omit the*
170 g/6 oz ricotta	*cumin and chilli)*

Make the batter by sieving the flour and salt into a mixing bowl. Make a well in the centre and break the eggs into it. Mix the eggs and flour together to achieve a smooth paste. Add the olive oil and then the mixed milk and water. Beat the batter with an egg whisk to get the air into it. Leave for 1–2 hours. Beat again before use.

Preheat the oven to 200°C/400°F/gas 6.

Meanwhile, make the stuffing by mixing all the ingredients

together except for the tomato sauce.

Make 13–15 cm/6–7 in pancakes, turning each one out on to absorbent paper. Fill each pancake with some of the stuffing and fold over like an envelope. Place the pancakes in a lightly greased baking dish and pour some of the prepared tomato sauce over each one. Bake in the oven for 10 minutes.

Lasagne verdi

Serves 6

Per serving: 480 kcal/34 g protein/19 g fat/47 g carbohydrate/ 22 g fibre

10 strips wholemeal lasagne
910 g/2 lb courgettes
910 g/2 lb spinach
910 g/2 lb fresh peas, podded
285 ml/½ pt semi-skimmed milk
2 eggs, beaten
seasoning
115 g/4 oz sage Derby cheese, grated

For the cheese sauce:
25 g/1 oz butter
55 g/2 oz plain flour
285 ml/½ pt semi-skimmed milk
85 g/3 oz mature Cheddar, grated
seasoning

Preheat the oven to 200°C/400°F/gas 6.

Boil the strips of lasagne in plenty of salted water for 10–15 minutes. When they are done, take each piece out separately and drain on tea towels. Choose a large, wide, shallow ovenproof dish. Butter it and lay two-thirds of the sheets of lasagne on the bottom and around the sides.

Slice the courgettes into rings and cook them with the spinach in their own juices for 10–12 minutes. Chop the cooked spinach with a wooden spoon and arrange it with the courgettes over the lasagne in the dish. Cook the podded peas in boiling water for about 8 minutes, drain and liquidize with the 285 ml/½ pt semi-skimmed milk and the eggs. Season. Sprinkle the grated sage Derby cheese over the spinach in the dish. Pour the liquidized pea mixture over the cheese and cover with the remaining pasta sheets.

Now prepare the sauce. Make a roux with the butter and flour. Gradually add the milk, stirring all the time. Add the Cheddar cheese. Season the sauce, which should be fairly thick. Pour the sauce over the top of the lasagne, ensuring that it is completely covered.

Place in the oven for 30 minutes, or until the top is brown and the interior is bubbling.

Note: If you cannot find sage Derby, use any hard cheese such as Cheddar and add a pinch of sage.

Lasagne verdi (*above*), Tagliatelle with eggs and herbs (*below*, see page 86)

French gnocchi

Serves 4
Per serving: 400 g kcal/17 g protein/18 g fat/45 g carbohydrate/
2 g fibre

285 ml/½ pt water	*115 g/4 oz plain flour*
25 g/1 oz butter	*4 eggs*
1 tsp sea salt	*45 g/1½ oz Parmesan, grated*
½ tsp black pepper	*45 g/1½ oz Gruyère, grated*
½ tsp grated nutmeg	*450 g/1 lb mashed potatoes*

Bring the water to the boil in a thick-bottomed saucepan. Add the butter, seasoning and nutmeg then pour in the flour. Take the saucepan off the heat and beat the mixture so that the flour and water amalgamate. Place back over the heat and continue to stir vigorously until the paste begins to leave the sides of the pan. Remove from the heat again and beat in the eggs, one by one. This is a *pâte à choux*. Now mix the Parmesan and Gruyère with the mashed potatoes and beat this mixture into the *pâte à choux*. Take spoonfuls of the mixture and roll out on a floured board.

Bring a large saucepan of salted water to the boil. Let it simmer and then throw in the gnocchi and poach them for 15 minutes. When they are done they should have doubled in size. The gnocchi must be well drained and may be served with tomato sauce (see page 76).

Herb gnocchi

Serves 4
Per serving: 440 kcal/17 g protein/23 g fat/45 g carbohydrate/
2 g fibre

To the above recipe add a generous handful of finely chopped parsley and mint at the same time as the cheeses and potatoes are beaten into the mixture. Serve the poached gnocchi with 25 g/1 oz of melted butter.

Gnocchi baked with cheese

Serves 4
Per serving: 445 kcal/20 g protein/22 g fat/45 g carbohydrate/
2 g fibre

Preheat the oven to 200°C/400°F/gas 6.

Follow the recipe for French gnocchi. When the gnocchi have been poached and drained, place them in a greased ovenproof dish and cover with 55 g/2 oz of mozzarella, thinly sliced. Bake for 10 minutes.

Riso verdi (*above*, see page 92), French gnocchi (*below*)

Indian rice   V

Serves 4   See photograph, page 78
**Per serving: 445 kcal/8 g protein/14 g fat/79 g carbohydrate/
4 g fibre**

340 g/12 oz long-grain rice	*1 tsp fenugreek*
pinch saffron	*1 tsp poppy seeds*
2 onions, finely sliced	*1 tbsp cashew nuts, chopped*
3 cloves garlic, crushed	*1 tbsp almonds, chopped*
55 g/2 oz ginger root, grated	*1 tbsp sultanas*
2 tbsp corn oil	*seasoning*
1 tsp cumin	*handful coriander leaves, chopped*
1 tsp fennel	

Boil the rice with the saffron until it is just cooked. In the mean-
time, cook the onions, garlic and ginger root in the corn oil. Add
all the spices then the nuts and sultanas. Cook for a few
minutes. Season.

When the rice is done, drain it well, then stir into the nut and
spice mixture with the coriander leaves. Serve.

Riso verdi   (V)

Serves 4   See photograph, page 90
**Per serving: 490 kcal/15 g protein/14 g fat/77 g carbohydrate/
13 g fibre**

285 g/10 oz long-grain rice	*bunch parsley, finely chopped*
450 g/1 lb fresh peas	*55 g/2 oz pistachio nuts, shelled*
450 g/1 lb mangetout	*85 ml/3 fl oz dry vermouth*
25 g/1 oz butter	*seasoning*

Cook the rice then drain well and place in a warm oven to dry out.
Pod the fresh peas and slice the mangetout. Cook these in a little
water until tender. Drain well. Melt the butter and mix with the
peas, mangetout, parsley and pistachio nuts. Stir this mixture into
the rice. Mix well. Pour the vermouth over the rice, season and
leave the rice in a warm oven for 2–3 minutes before serving.

Beetroot and ginger rice   (V)

Serves 4
**Per serving: 295 kcal/9 g protein/6 g fat/55 g carbohydrate/
9 g fibre**

450 g/1 lb raw beetroot	*170 g/6 oz long-grain rice*
1 small cabbage	*25 g/1 oz butter*
55 g/2 oz ginger root	*2 extra beetroot, peeled and grated*
salt	

Preheat the oven to 150°C/325°F/gas 3.

Peel and chop 450 g/1 lb beetroot coarsely and place in a large casserole. Chop the cabbage and the ginger and add to the beetroot in the casserole. Pour on enough boiling water to cover the vegetables. Add a little salt and place in the oven for 3–4 hours.

Remove the casserole from the oven and drain all the liquid from the vegetables. Reserve the liquid and discard the vegetables. Boil the rice in the beetroot stock. When it is cooked the rice should have absorbed all the liquid. Stir the butter into the rice and then add the 2 extra beetroot, peeled and grated. This dish can be eaten hot or cold.

Vegetable risotto

Serves 4
Per serving: 445 kcal/14 g protein/14 g fat/70 g carbohydrate/ 8 g fibre

2 courgettes	*400 g/14 oz can tomatoes*
2 onions	*1 tbsp tomato purée*
450 g/1 lb mushrooms	*seasoning*
1 tbsp olive oil	*generous handful fresh parsley, finely*
5 cloves garlic, crushed	*chopped*
285 g/10 oz long-grain rice	*55 g/2 oz Parmesan, grated*
145 ml/5 fl oz red wine	*25 g/1 oz butter*

Preheat the oven to 175°C/350°F/gas 4.

Chop the courgettes, slice the onions and mushrooms. Heat the oil in a heavy pan and sauté the courgettes, onions and mushrooms with the garlic for a few moments. Add the rice and cook for a further minute or two, stirring all the time. Now add the red wine, the canned tomatoes and the tomato purée. Season. Add enough water just to cover the rice. Place in the oven for 30–40 minutes.

When the risotto is cooked, add the parsley and grated Parmesan, stir in the butter and serve.

Suppli

The best supper dish if you have any leftover risotto.

Mix a handful of fresh herbs, finely chopped, into the cold risotto. Make small croquettes with the risotto, placing slices of mozzarella cheese inside. Dip the croquettes in beaten egg, then roll them in fine wholemeal breadcrumbs. Fry them in hot olive oil.

Pizza

Serves 4
Per serving: 415 kcal/10 g protein/18 g fat/57 g carbohydrate/
5 g fibre

For the dough:
225 g/8 oz strong white flour
½ tsp salt
15 g/½ oz fresh yeast
2 tbsp warmed milk
1 egg, beaten
2 tbsp olive oil
2–3 tbsp warm water

For the filling:
2 onions

1 pepper
2 tbsp olive oil
5 cloves garlic, crushed
1 tsp oregano
400 g/14 oz can tomatoes
2 tbsp tomato purée
seasoning
5 fresh tomatoes, sliced
12 black olives, stoned
2 tbsp capers

Sieve the flour and the salt into a large mixing bowl. Place the yeast in a cup and pour the warmed milk over it. Stir and leave to ferment – about 10 minutes. Once fermented, add the creamed yeast to the flour then add the beaten egg, olive oil and warm water. Stir well. Start to work the dough with your hands. Knead it until it becomes smooth and elastic. Form the dough into a ball and leave in a covered bowl in a warm place for 2 hours to allow it to rise.

Preheat the oven to 218°C/425°F/gas 7.

While the dough is rising, make the filling. Slice the onions and the pepper. Heat the olive oil in a pan and add the onions, pepper, garlic and oregano. Cook them gently for about 10 minutes, then add the canned tomatoes. Simmer the mixture for 45 minutes, by which time you should have a thick sauce. Add the tomato purée and seasoning and cook for another 5 minutes.

Oil a 30 x 45 cm/12 x 14 in baking sheet. Take your ball of risen dough and smooth it down over the baking sheet, pressing and pulling the dough out. Make a small ridge of dough around the edge of the sheet. Leave to rest for 10 minutes. Smear the filling over the dough then garnish with slices of fresh tomato, the black olives and capers. Rest the pizza again for another 10 minutes.

Bake the pizza in the preheated oven for 15 minutes, then turn the oven down to 175°C/350°F/gas 4 for another 15 minutes.

Pizza filling II: Tomato and chilli

Total pizza serves 4
Per serving: 490 kcal/19 g protein/23 g fat/55 g carbohydrate/
5 g fibre

1 tbsp olive oil
2 onions, finely chopped

3 cloves garlic, crushed
2 tsp dried oregano

800 g/1 lb 12 oz can tomatoes *3 tbsp tomato purée*
3 dried red chillis *115 g/4 oz mozzarella, sliced*
seasoning

Heat the oil in a pan and add the onions, garlic and oregano. Cook gently for 5 minutes. Next add the canned tomatoes and the chillis. Cook for 30 minutes. Season, add the tomato purée and cook for a further 5 minutes. Discard the dried chillis before spreading the filling over the pizza base, prepared as above. Bake as above, adding the mozzarella halfway through the cooking time.

Pizza filling III: Mushroom and artichoke

Total pizza serves 4
Per serving: 480 kcal/19 g protein/15 g fat/52 g carbohydrate/ 6 g fibre

1 tbsp olive oil *4 tbsp tomato purée*
1 tsp dried oregano *seasoning*
3 cloves garlic, crushed *3–4 canned artichoke hearts*
2 onions, sliced *115 g/4 oz mozzarella, sliced*
340 g/12 oz mushrooms, sliced

Heat the oil and add the oregano, garlic, onions and mushrooms. Cook gently for 10 minutes before adding the tomato purée and seasoning. Smear the filling over the pizza base, prepared as above. Slice the artichoke hearts thinly and arrange them over the pizza. Bake as above, adding the mozzarella halfway through the cooking time.

VEGETABLE DISHES

One of the great charms of vegetarian cooking is that no food, dish or meal is confined within a straightjacket. Some of the following recipes could be for a main course, for example, the stuffed cabbage, yet served to a larger group it would make an excellent beginning to a meal. Other recipes are side dishes, but would make equally delicious light suppers or lunches, like the potato and pepper gratin.

Vegetarian food need never be bland, but to get the full flavour from spices, make sure they are fresh. Always throw away any which have been kept longer than a few months. Keep spices away from the light and make sure they are tightly stoppered. Try to use herbs straight from the garden or the window box. Cook dishes seasonally, thus ensuring that you get the best use from fresh vegetables, though most of us are lucky now and can also cook with the many types of imported vegetables. Avoid buying those which seem limp or bruised – the flavour is generally feeble (apart from the vitamins being lost).

Artichoke stew (V)

Serves 4
Per serving: 190 kcal/10 g protein/6 g fat/26 g carbohydrate/ 10 g fibre

12 baby globe artichokes	450 g/1 lb fresh peas, podded
1.45l/2½ pt water	25 g/1 oz butter
2 green peppers	25 g/1 oz plain flour
450 g/1 lb baby carrots	seasoning

Trim the artichokes and discard any tough outer leaves. Quarter them and boil in the water for 5 minutes. Core and deseed the peppers and slice the carrots thinly. Add these to the artichokes in their water and simmer for another 15 minutes. Add the podded peas and cook for a further 10 minutes.

Melt the butter in pan and add the flour to make a roux. Drain the vegetables, retaining the stock and returning the vegetables to their saucepan. Add enough of the stock to the roux to make a thin sauce. Season and pour the sauce over the drained vegetables in their saucepan. Reheat very carefully over a gentle heat before serving.

Artichoke soufflé

Serves 4   See photograph, page 99
Per serving: 230 kcal/17 g protein/15 g fat/8 g carbohydrate/
10 g fibre

4 large globe artichokes	*285 ml/½ pt skimmed milk*
5 eggs	*seasoning*
55 g/2 oz Gruyère	

Preheat the oven to 200°C/400°F/gas 6.

Boil the artichokes in plenty of water for 45 minutes. Drain and leave to cool. Scrape the flesh from the bottom of each artichoke leaf into a mixing bowl. With a sharp knife, dig out the hairy choke from each artichoke and discard, then dice the pad of flesh which is at the bottom of the artichoke. Add the diced flesh to the bowl.

Separate the eggs and add the yolks to the artichoke flesh with the Gruyère and the skimmed milk. Purée. Whip up the egg whites until they are stiff. Butter a soufflé dish. Fold the egg whites into the artichoke mixture and gently pour into the soufflé dish.

Bake the soufflé for 20 minutes or until the top is well risen and brown. Serve immediately. The centre and bottom of the soufflé should still be liquid.

Broccoli with Maltese sauce

Serves 6   See photograph, page 101
Per serving: 250 kcal/9 g protein/20 g fat/9 g carbohydrate/
8 g fibre

1.15 kg/2½ lb broccoli	*pinch cayenne pepper*
2 oranges, preferably blood oranges	*seasoning*
115 g/4 oz unsalted butter	*3 egg yolks*

Cut and trim the broccoli and steam it for 5–6 minutes or until it is just cooked. Meanwhile take the zest from the oranges and then squeeze them. Add the zest to the juice and pour it into a pan. Melt the butter in the orange juice, adding the cayenne pepper and seasoning.

Place the egg yolks in a blender jar and, very slowly, pour the butter and orange mixture on to the egg yolks, blending all the time, until the mixture becomes a hollandaise sauce – but flavoured with blood oranges.

Place the broccoli in a warm dish and pour the sauce over.

Baked fennel (V)

Serves 4
Per serving: 155 kcal/9 g protein/12 g fat/3 g carbohydrate/
4 g fibre

4 fennel roots   *a little butter*
55 g/2 oz Parmesan, grated

Preheat the oven to 175°C/350°F/gas 4.
  Trim the fennel roots and slice them into halves. Boil in lightly
salted water for 10 minutes. Drain well. Place the fennel in a
greased ovenproof dish and sprinkle the Parmesan over the top.
Give the dish several grinds from the black pepper mill, dot with
butter and bake in the oven for 10 minutes.

Baked parsnips with pine nuts (V)

Serves 4   See photograph, page 100
Per serving: 170 kcal/4 g protein/9 g fat/20 g carbohydrate/
7 g fibre

675 g/1 lb 8 oz parsnips   *seasoning*
25 g/1 oz butter or margarine   *25 g/1 oz pine nuts*

Preheat the oven to 200°C/400°F/gas 6.
  Peel and chop the parsnips. Boil them in salted water for 10
minutes or until they are soft. Drain them well, then blend them
to a purée with the butter and seasoning. Place the parsnips in an
ovenproof dish.
  Roast the pine nuts on a baking tray until they are golden
brown, then sprinkle over the top of the parsnips. Place the dish in
the oven to reheat for 5 minutes.

Stuffed aubergines [V]

Serves 4
Per serving: 135 kcal/3 g protein/8 g fat/14 g carbohydrate/
5 g fibre

2 aubergines   *½ tsp ground cumin*
2 tbsp olive oil   *½ tsp garam masala*
2 onions, sliced   *85 g/3 oz mashed potatoes*
2 courgettes, sliced   *2 tomatoes, peeled and diced*
3 cloves garlic, crushed   *1 tbsp tomato purée*
½ tsp paprika   *seasoning*
½ tsp ground ginger   *2 tbsp green coriander, finely chopped*

Artichoke soufflé (see page 97);
OVERLEAF: Baked parsnips with pine nuts (*left*, see page 98), Leek
timbale (*centre*, see page 105), Broccoli with Maltese sauce (*right*, see
page 97)

Preheat the oven to 190°C/375°F/gas 5.

Halve the aubergines and boil them for 5 minutes. Drain well. Scoop out the centre flesh, leaving 5 mm/¼ in around the sides, next to the skin. Dice the flesh you have removed.

Heat the oil in a pan and cook the sliced onions and courgettes with the garlic and spices for about 5 minutes, until they are soft. Add the potatoes and the aubergine flesh then the tomatoes and the tomato purée. Mix thoroughly, season and cook for a few more minutes.

Pile the stuffing into the aubergine boats. Place them in a greased ovenproof dish and bake in the oven for 20 minutes. Sprinkle the chopped coriander over the top before serving.

Stuffed cabbage

Makes 12 stuffed leaves
Per leaf: 125 kcal/4 g protein/9 g fat/8 g carbohydrate/3 g fibre

12 large leaves of a Savoy cabbage	*170 g/6 oz ricotta*
2 peppers, sliced	*55 g/2 oz wholemeal breadcrumbs*
2 onions, sliced	*55 g/2 oz broken walnuts*
2 tbsp olive oil	*seasoning*
1 tsp oregano	*570 ml/1 pt vegetable stock (see*
1 tsp dill weed	*page 46)*

Cut away the roughest part of the stalk at the bottom of the cabbage leaves, blanch them and drain them well. Heat the olive oil in a pan and cook the peppers and onions, adding the oregano and dill weed. When they are soft, pour into a mixing bowl and add the ricotta, breadcrumbs and walnuts. Mix thoroughly and season.

Take the cabbage leaves one by one. Place a little of the stuffing on each leaf and roll up, tucking the corners in. Put the cabbage parcels in the bottom of a large saucepan, wedging them up against each other. Pour the vegetable stock into the pan and bring to the boil. Simmer for 20 minutes. Drain and serve.

Stuffed peppers

Serves 4
Per serving: 305 kcal/13 g protein/19 g fat/22 g carbohydrate/ 5 g fibre

4 large peppers	*generous handful parsley, chopped*
85 g/3 oz wholemeal breadcrumbs	*dash Tabasco sauce*
2 large onions, finely chopped	*225 g/8 oz ricotta*
3 cloves garlic, crushed	*2 eggs*
10 black olives, stoned and chopped	*seasoning*
2 tbsp capers	

Stuffed peppers and Stuffed cabbage

Preheat the oven to 175°C/350°F/gas 4.

Slice the tops off the peppers and reserve. Core and deseed the main part of the peppers and set aside. Mix the remaining ingredients together and fill the peppers with the stuffing.

Select a casserole dish in which the peppers can fit, wedged together, standing upright. Pour about 2.5 cm/1 in water in the bottom of the dish around the bottoms of the peppers. Fit the tops of the peppers back on. Put the lid on the casserole and bake in the oven for 40 minutes.

Potato and pepper gratin

Serves 4
Per serving: 305 kcal/8 g protein/14 g fat/40 g carbohydrate/ 5 g fibre

675 g/1 lb 8 oz potatoes	*3 tbsp olive oil*
4 peppers	*3 cloves garlic, crushed*
1 onion	*seasoning*
25 g/1 oz butter	*25 g/1 oz Parmesan, grated*

Preheat the oven to 175°C/350°F/gas 4.

Peel the potatoes and boil them for 15 minutes. Drain and slice them. Core and deseed the peppers. Slice them with the onion. Melt the butter and oil in a pan and add the peppers, onion, potatoes and garlic. Season the dish and cook for 5 minutes. Turn out into a gratin dish. Sprinkle with the Parmesan and bake in the oven for 10 minutes.

Potato tarkari Ⓥ

Serves 4
Per serving: 250 kcal/4 g protein/11 g fat/37 g carbohydrate/ 3 g fibre

675 g/1 lb 8 oz potatoes	*½ tsp paprika*
2 onions, sliced	*½ tsp fenugreek*
3 tbsp sunflower oil	*½ tsp mustard seeds*
55 g/2 oz ginger root, grated	*seasoning*
2 tbsp green peppercorns	*2 tbsp coriander leaves, chopped*

Boil the potatoes for 15 minutes. Drain well and dice them. Heat the oil in a heavy pan and add the onions, ginger root, peppercorns and spices. Cook for a few minutes before adding the diced potatoes and seasoning. Put a lid over the pan and cook for 10 minutes. Remove the lid, raise the heat and brown the potatoes. Sprinkle with coriander leaves before serving.

Potato and spinach pie

Serves 4
Per serving: 300 kcal/18 g protein/8 g fat/43 g carbohydrate/
12 g fibre

25 g/1 oz butter	seasoning
675 g/1 lb 8 oz spinach	1 egg
675 g/1 lb 8 oz potatoes	570 ml/1 pt skimmed milk
pinch grated nutmeg	

Preheat the oven to 150°C/325°F/gas 3.

Melt the butter in a saucepan and cook the spinach in the butter, with the lid on, until its bulk is reduced by two-thirds – about 10 minutes. Chop the cooked spinach with a wooden spoon and tip into a deep pie dish. Peel and slice the potatoes. Leave the slices to soak in cold water for 30 minutes to rid them of some of their starch. Rinse and drain well. Pat the potato slices dry and arrange them over the spinach, sprinkling each layer with a little nutmeg and seasoning.

Beat the egg into the skimmed milk and pour the mixture over the top of the potatoes. Let the liquid seep down into the dish before baking in the oven for 2 hours.

Leek timbale

Serves 4   **See photograph, page 100**
Per serving: 275 kcal/15 g protein/16 g fat/19 g carbohydrate/
5 g fibre

450 g/1 lb leeks	pinch grated nutmeg
25 g/1 oz butter or margarine	seasoning
5 eggs	55 g/2 oz wholemeal breadcrumbs
25 g/1 oz Gruyère	285 ml/½ pt semi-skimmed milk

Preheat the oven to 175°C/350°F/gas 4.

Wash and slice the leeks. Cook them with the butter in a pan over a low heat with the lid tightly on. They should be cooked through in 5–8 minutes. Leave to cool then place in a blender with the eggs and reduce to a purée. Pour the purée into a mixing bowl and add the Gruyère, nutmeg and seasoning.

Butter a mould or soufflé dish. Pour the breadcrumbs into the prepared mould so that the breadcrumbs stick to the bottom and sides. Shake out any loose breadcrumbs into the leek purée.

Heat the milk almost to boiling point and pour it slowly into the leek purée, beating as you pour. Tip the mixture into the mould or soufflé dish slowly, so that you don't disturb the breadcrumbs.

Stand the dish in a baking tin filled with boiling water and place in the oven for 45 minutes, or until set firm. Remove the timbale from the oven and let it rest for 5 minutes before unmoulding on to a platter. Pour a tomato sauce (see page 76) or mushroom sauce (see page 85) around the base and serve.

Pumpkin and tomato casserole (V)

Serves 4
Per serving: 140 kcal/3 g protein/9 g fat/13 g carbohydrate/ 7 g fibre

910 g/2 lb tomatoes
3 cloves garlic, crushed
generous bunch fresh basil, chopped
1 tbsp olive oil

25 g/1 oz butter or margarine
675 g/1 lb 8 oz pumpkin flesh,
  cubed
seasoning

Preheat the oven to 175°C/350°F/gas 4.
  Cook the tomatoes with the garlic, basil and oil in a saucepan with a closely fitting lid for 10 minutes. Leave to cool, then put through a sieve. Reserve the tomato sauce, but discard the skins and debris. Melt the butter in a flameproof casserole. Fry the cubed pumpkin flesh for about 5 minutes. Add the tomato sauce and seasoning. Bake in the oven for 15 minutes.

Winter casserole (V)

Serves 6
Per serving: 250 kcal/7 g protein/11 g fat/33 g carbohydrate/ 8 g fibre

450 g/1 lb potatoes
1.15 1/2 pt vegetable stock (see page
  46)
25 g/1 oz butter
1 tbsp olive oil
450 g/1 lb carrots, chopped
450 g/1 lb turnips, chopped
1 head celery, chopped

145 ml/5 fl oz shoyu sauce (available
  from Chinese stores)
1 tbsp French mustard
25 g/1 oz softened butter
25 g/1 oz plain flour
seasoning
1 bunch parsley, finely chopped

Preheat the oven to 175°C/350°F/gas 4.
  Peel and chop the potatoes. Cook them in a large pan with the vegetable stock for 10 minutes. Melt the butter in the olive oil in a casserole and add the chopped carrots, turnips and celery. Let them cook for a moment before adding the potatoes in their stock. Mix in the shoyu sauce and mustard and place in the oven for 30 minutes.
  Meanwhile mix the softened butter with the flour to form a paste.
  Remove the casserole from the oven when the cooking time is up. Check for seasoning. Add small pellets of the flour paste to the casserole, stirring vigorously, until the sauce thickens. At the last minute stir in the chopped parsley.

FRUIT DISHES

The best and most healthy conclusion to a meal is fresh fruit, with nothing added to it at all. But sometimes our palates demand something more enticing, and certainly in summer when soft fruits are in season a range of fruit salads made from these can hardly be bettered. There are no recipes for fruit salads because they are simply created from the best of the seasonal fruits, but it is as well to remember never to peel fruits and always to use them as fresh as possible. The other controversial issue is how much to sweeten. All sugars are equally bad for us in that they are a cause of tooth decay and a large contributory factor to obesity. Fresh fruit should be sweet enough, but if not, fruit salads can be marinated in apple juice or a little concentrated orange juice.

In this section I have tended to give a lot of recipes using dried apricots and other dried fruits. This is because dried apricots are a rich source of dietary fibre, minerals and vitamins. They are also astonishingly delicious and sweet in themselves. When buying dried fruits, go for the best. It pays to buy the most expensive, for a little goes a long way. Dried fruits also make a stunning combination with nuts as in the Syrian fruit salad (page 110).

Apricot and almond purée (V)

Serves 4
Per serving: 315 kcal/8 g protein/20 g fat/28 g carbohydrate/ 18 g fibre

225 g/8 oz dried apricots   *1 tbsp honey (optional)*
55 g/2 oz ground almonds   *55 g/2 oz flaked almonds*
25 g/1 oz butter

Soak the apricots overnight. Simmer them in the water they were soaked in for 10 minutes. Leave to cool, then blend to a purée with the ground almonds, butter and honey (if using). Place the flaked almonds in a saucepan and heat so that they brown slightly. Empty the purée into a bowl and decorate with the flaked almonds.

Apricot and walnut fool

Serves 4
Per serving: 450 kcal/16 g protein/14 g fat/38 g carbohydrate/ 17 g fibre

285 g/10 oz dried apricots   *145 ml/5 fl oz Jamaican rum*
25 g/1 oz raisins   *145 ml/5 fl oz dry sherry*

285 ml/½ pt low fat quark   *85 g/3 oz broken walnuts*

Soak the apricots overnight in water and soak the raisins overnight in the rum. Simmer the apricots in their water for 10 minutes. When they are cooked, blend to a purée with the sherry and quark. Pour the purée into a dish and cover with the raisins and their juice. Sprinkle the walnuts over the top and chill for an hour before serving.

Baked apples with apricots   (V)

Serves 4
Per serving: 220 kcal/3 g protein/5 g fat/44 g carbohydrate/
15 g fibre

8 dried apricots   *55 g/2 oz ground almonds*
4 large cooking apples   *1 tbsp honey (optional)*
25 g/1 oz butter

Preheat the oven to 200°C/400°F/gas 6.
   Soak the apricots overnight in water. Core the apples. Mix the butter, almonds and honey (if using) together. Chop the soaked apricots and add these to the mixture. Stuff the centre of the apples with the mixture. Place in a baking dish in the oven for 20–30 minutes.

Baked apples with lemon and walnuts

Serves 4   (V)
Per serving: 220 kcal/2 g protein/12 g fat/28 g carbohydrate/
7 g fibre

4 large cooking apples   *1 tbsp honey (optional)*
juice and zest of 1 lemon   *55 g/2 oz ground walnuts*
25 g/1 oz butter   *4 walnut halves*

Preheat the oven to 200°C/400°F/gas 6.
   Core the apples and place them in a baking dish. Mix the lemon zest, juice, butter, honey (if using) and ground walnuts until you have a smooth paste. Fill the apples with the mixture and bake in the oven for 20–30 minutes.
   Decorate with the walnut halves before serving.

Apple and nut salad

Serves 4
Per serving: 250 kcal/5 g protein/18 g fat/18 g carbohydrate/
5 g fibre

4 dessert apples	*1 tbsp honey*
55 g/2 oz walnuts	*1 tbsp walnut oil*
55 g/2 oz flaked almonds	*2 tbsp Greek yogurt*

Core the apples and slice thinly. Place in a large bowl and mix in
the walnuts and almonds. Mix the honey, walnut oil and Greek
yogurt together and dribble over the salad. Toss thoroughly
before serving.

Melon stuffed with raspberry cream

Serves 4   See photograph, page 111
Per serving: 155 kcal/13 g protein/3 g fat/21 g carbohydrate/
10 g fibre

½ Ogen melon per person	*1 tbsp honey (optional)*
450 g/1 lb fresh raspberries	
285 ml/½ pt fromage frais or low	
fat quark	

Slice the melons in half and deseed them. Chill. Mix the
raspberries with the fromage frais or quark and add the honey if
you think the mixture isn't sweet enough. Fill the melons with the
raspberry cream and chill for 1 hour before serving.

Nectarines and strawberries in red wine V

Serves 6
Per serving: 110 kcal/2 g protein/negligible fat/18 g carbohydrate/
4 g fibre

6 nectarines	*285 ml/½ pt red wine*
450 g/1 lb strawberries	

Halve the nectarines and remove the stones. Place in a bowl. Hull
the strawberries and add them to the nectarines. Pour the wine
over the fruit and leave for half a day.

Marinaded oranges ☑

Serves 4
Per serving: 170 kcal/2 g protein/negligible fat/30 g carbohydrate/
4 g fibre

6 large oranges   *2 tbsp apple juice*
145 ml/5 fl oz Cointreau

Grate the zest from the oranges, then peel them ensuring that all
the pith comes away from the flesh. Slice them across thinly and
lay them in a bowl with the zest. Pour the Cointreau and apple
juice over them. Leave for half a day and chill before serving.

Syrian fruit salad ☑

Serves 6
Per serving: 220 kcal/4 g protein/8 g fat/36 g carbohydrate/
12 g fibre

85 g/3 oz dried apricots   *2 tbsp flaked almonds*
85 g/3 oz dried figs   *2 tbsp broken walnuts*
85 g/3 oz dried peaches   *2 tbsp pine nuts*
55 g/2 oz prunes   *2 tbsp honey*
2 tbsp raisins   *2 tbsp rose water*
2 tbsp sultanas

Place all the dried fruits in a large bowl. Cover with water and soak
overnight. In the morning stone the prunes and chop all the fruit.
Return to the water in which the fruit was soaked and add the rest
of the ingredients. Leave for another 24 hours before serving.

Marinaded dried fruits ☑

Serves 4
Per serving: 270 kcal/2 g protein/negligible fat/37 g carbohydrate/
12 g fibre

85 g/3 oz dried apricots   *1 tbsp concentrated orange juice*
85 g/3 oz dried peaches   *145 ml/5 fl oz ginger wine*
85 g/3 oz dried figs   *145 ml/5 fl oz brandy*

Place all the dried fruits in a large bowl and add the rest of the
ingredients. Add enough water to cover the fruit. Leave for 24
hours then chop the fruit coarsely and return to the marinade for
another day before serving.

Syrian fruit salad (*top*), Apricot and ginger tart (*centre*, see page 113),
Melon stuffed with raspberry cream (*bottom*, see page 109)

Brandied apricots   Ⅴ

Serves 4
Per serving: 420 kcal/6 g protein/negligible fat/63 g carbohydrate/
27 g fibre

450 g/1 lb dried apricots   145 ml/5 fl oz water
85 g/3 oz raw cane sugar   285 ml/½ pt brandy

Place the apricots in a glass jar with a close fitting lid. Boil the
sugar and water together to make a syrup. Pour the syrup into the
jar over the apricots, then pour in the brandy. Screw on the lid of
the jar very tightly and leave in a cool dark place for 1 month.
  Once the apricots have soaked up the liquid the jar may need
topping up with brandy, so check them every so often.

Peach tart   (V)

Makes 6 slices
Per slice: 260 kcal/4 g protein/10 g fat/41 g carbohydrate/5 g fibre

115 g/4 oz dried peaches   145 ml/5 fl oz water
20–20.5 cm/8–9 in wholemeal pastry   2 tbsp raw cane sugar
  case, baked blind (see page 64)   4 fresh peaches

Soak the dried peaches overnight, then simmer them in their
soaking water for 10 minutes before blending them to a thick
purée.
  Fill the cool pastry case with the peach purée. Heat the water
and sugar in a pan to make a syrup. Slice the fresh peaches in half
and remove the stones. Poach the peaches in the syrup for 5
minutes. Remove the peaches from the syrup and lay them in the
peach purée. Glaze with the syrup.

Apricot and ginger tart   (V)

Makes 6 slices   See photograph, page 111
Per slice: 380 kcal/5 g protein/19 g fat/52 g carbohydrate/8 g fibre

225 g/8 oz dried apricots   20–22.5 cm/8–9 in wholemeal pastry
55 g/2 oz ground almonds   case, baked blind (see page 64)
25 g/1 oz butter   115 g/4 oz stem ginger in syrup

Make an apricot purée following the method on page 107. Fill the
cool pastry case with the purée. Slice the stem ginger and
decorate the purée with overlapping slices. Dribble some of the
syrup over the top and chill before serving.

Indian mixed pickle (*top*, see page 119), Blue cheese (*centre*, see page
116), Parsley cheese (*bottom*, see page 115)

Spiced fig tart   (V)

Makes 6 slices
Per slice: 295 kcal/5 g protein/13 g fat/38 g carbohydrate/9 g fibre

225 g/8 oz dried figs
145 ml/5 fl oz white wine
pinch each:
  cloves
  mace
  ginger
  cinnamon

1 tbsp each:
  raisins
  sultanas
  currants
55 g/2 oz ground almonds
20–20.5 cm/8–9 in wholemeal pastry
  case, baked blind (see page 64)
1 tbsp blanched almonds

Soak the figs overnight. Simmer them in their water with the white wine and spices for 10 minutes. Leave to cool before blending them into a purée with the raisins, sultanas, currants and ground almonds.

Fill the cool pastry case with the purée. Arrange the blanched almonds on the top.

Apple and chestnut tart   (V)

Makes 8 slices
Per slice: 325 kcal/4 g protein/13 g fat/51 g carbohydrate/9 g fibre

20–20.5 cm/8–9 in wholemeal pastry
  case baked blind (see page 64)
450 g/1 lb can of chestnut purée
1 large cooking apple

55 g/2 oz candied orange and lemon
  peel
55 g/2 oz blanched almonds
zest and juice of 1 lemon

Fill the cool pastry case with the chestnut purée. Peel and core the apples and slice them. Arrange the slices over the purée. Sprinkle the candied peel and blanched almonds over the top of the apples, then sprinkle with the zest and juice of the lemon.

Heat the oven to 200°C/400°F/gas 6 and bake the tart for 15 minutes.

CHEESES, SAVOURIES AND PICKLES

Here are a few suggestions for finishing a meal, though some may make a snack or light lunch. We too easily neglect the low fat cheeses, finding them rather bland, so here are ways of brightening them up. The savouries can double for supper dishes.

We also tend to be too conservative in making pickles. Most vegetables take very kindly to being flavoured in pickling mixture with garlic and ginger. I find malt vinegar too vicious a flavour, destroying the natural flavour of the vegetables themselves. Cider or wine vinegar should always be used instead.

Parsley cheese   See photograph, page 112

Total recipe: 615 kcal/22 g protein/58 g fat/2 g carbohydrate/ 5 g fibre

handful fresh parsley   *seasoning*
225 g/8 oz curd cheese   *25 g/1 oz rolled oats*

Finely chop the parsley and add it to the curd cheese. Mix thoroughly and season. Roast the oats in a dry saucepan over a strong heat until they have turned golden brown. Shape the cheese into a round cake and roll in the oats. Chill well before serving.

Chive cheese

Total recipe: 690 kcal/22 g protein/58 g fat/19 g carbohydrate/ 5 g fibre

handful chives   *seasoning*
225 g/8 oz curd cheese   *25 g/1 oz buckwheat*

Chop the chives finely. Mix with the curd cheese and season. In a dry saucepan roast the buckwheat over a strong heat until it is golden brown. Shape the cheese into a round cake and roll in the wheat. Chill before serving.

Note: Buckwheat is also sold as bulgar wheat or cracked wheat.

Blue cheese
See photograph, page 112

**Total recipe: 1010 kcal/37 g protein/93 g fat/7 g carbohydrate/
1 g fibre**

55 g/2 oz Roquefort
225 g/8 oz curd cheese
handful mint

freshly ground black pepper
25 g/1 oz sesame seeds

Mix the Roquefort and the curd cheese thoroughly. Chop the mint finely and add to the cheese with the black pepper. Shape the cheese into a cake. Roast the sesame seeds in a dry pan over a strong heat until golden brown. Roll the cheese in the roasted seeds and chill before serving.

Soft cheese with walnuts

**Total recipe: 1000 kcal/24 g protein/99 g fat/4 g carbohydrate/
3 g fibre**

1 tbsp walnut oil
225 g/8 oz ricotta
55 g/2 oz broken walnuts

seasoning
2 tbsp green peppercorns

Add the oil to the ricotta and mix thoroughly. Chop the walnuts so that they are in very small pieces and add them to the ricotta. Season. Shape the cheese into a cake and roll it in the green peppercorns.

Liptauer

**Total recipe: 435 kcal/26 g protein/34 g fat/7 g carbohydrate/
2 g fibre**

115 g/4 oz ricotta
115 g/4 oz low fat quark
1 tbsp paprika
1 bunch spring onions, chopped

1 tbsp capers
1 tbsp chopped gherkins
seasoning

Mix all the ingredients together and place in a bowl. Chill well before serving.

Toasted bean purée

Serves 4
**Per serving: 275 kcal/14 g protein/14 g fat/25 g carbohydrate/
7 g fibre**

4 slices wholemeal bread, toasted
6 tbsp flageolet purée (see page 35)

8 slices mozzarella
1 tsp paprika

Spread the hot toast with the purée and place it under the hot grill for a few minutes. Next cover the purée with 2 slices of mozzarella per slice of toast and return to the grill. When the cheese has melted sprinkle with a little paprika and serve.

Avocado toast

Serves 4
Per serving: 165 kcal/5 g protein/6 g fat/24 g carbohydrate/ 7 g fibre

6 tbsp avocado sauce (see page 38) *4 tomatoes, sliced*
4 slices wholemeal bread, toasted *1 tbsp capers*

Spread the avocado sauce on to the toast. Cover with the slices of tomato and a few capers. Place under a hot grill for a few minutes.

Stuffed mushrooms

Serves 4
Per serving: 185 kcal/9 g protein/13 g fat/9 g carbohydrate/ 3 g fibre

4 large mushrooms *55 g/2 oz curd cheese*
25 g/1 oz butter *55 g/2 oz Parmesan, grated*
55 g/2 oz wholemeal breadcrumbs *handful parsley, finely chopped*
3 cloves garlic, crushed *seasoning*

Preheat the oven to 200°C/400°F/gas 6.

Wipe the mushrooms but do not peel. Remove the stalks and, if they are not too fibrous, chop them finely. Melt the butter in a pan and add the mushroom stalks. Cook them for a few minutes until they are soft. Pour into a bowl and add the breadcrumbs, garlic, cheeses, parsley and seasoning. Mix well.

Fill the upturned mushrooms with the stuffing. Place them in a buttered ovenproof dish and bake in the oven for 10 minutes. Serve hot.

Parmesan croûtes

Serves 4
Per serving: 385 kcal/18 g protein/26 g fat/21 g carbohydrate/ 4 g fibre

85 g/3 oz Parmesan, grated *seasoning*
85 g/3 oz Gruyère, grated *4 slices wholemeal bread, toasted*
55 g/2 oz butter, softened

Mix the cheeses, butter and seasoning together thoroughly. Spread the mixture on to the hot toast and place under a hot grill until the cheese is melted and bubbling. Serve at once.

Macaroni croquettes

Serves 4
Per serving: 490 kcal/18 g protein/23 g fat/56 g carbohydrate/ 8 g fibre

225 g/8 oz wholemeal macaroni	*seasoning*
25 g/1 oz butter	*1 egg, beaten*
25 g/1 oz plain flour	*55 g/2 oz wholemeal breadcrumbs*
285 ml/½ pt semi-skimmed milk	*corn oil for frying*
55 g/2 oz mature Cheddar, grated	

Cook the macaroni in plenty of lightly salted boiling water for about 5 minutes. When it is *al dente*, drain and cut into small pieces. Melt the butter in a pan, add the flour and make a roux. Gradually stir in the milk. Add the cheese and seasoning to make a thick sauce. Let the sauce cool, then stir in the chopped macaroni.

Shape the mixture into small croquettes. Dip them into the beaten egg and then roll them in the breadcrumbs. Heat the oil and fry the croquettes until they are golden brown.

Pickled onions   [V]

Total recipe: 315 kcal/12 g protein/negligible fat/71 g carbo- hydrate/18 g fibre

1.35 kg/3 lb pickling onions	*25 g/1 oz pickling spices*
55 g/2 oz sea salt	*85 g/3 oz ginger root*
570 ml/1 pt water	*2 dried red chillis*
1 1/1 pt 15 fl oz cider vinegar	

Blanch the onions in boiling water for a few minutes. They will now peel easily. Dissolve the salt in the water to make a brine solution. Place the peeled onions in the brine and leave for 24 hours.

Heat the vinegar, adding the spices, peeled and sliced ginger root and the chillis. Choose a clean glass jar with a tightly fitting lid and sterilize it. Drain the onions, pack into the jar and cover with the vinegar and spices. Seal firmly and store for 6 months.

Indian mixed pickle [V]

See photograph, page 112
Total recipe: 440 kcal/50 g protein/negligible fat/62 g carbohydrate/59 g fibre

1 red cabbage	*1 tsp each:*
1 cauliflower	*cloves*
1 cucumber	*coriander*
225 g/8 oz French beans	*mustard seed*
225 g/8 oz pickling onions	*black peppercorns*
sea salt	*cayenne pepper*
5 cloves garlic	*1 tbsp turmeric*
55 g/2 oz ginger root	*1 tbsp allspice*
1 1/1 pt 15 fl oz cider vinegar	

Slice the red cabbage and the cauliflower. Cut the cucumber into chunks. Trim the French beans. Peel the onions. Place all the prepared vegetables in a large bowl and sprinkle salt over them. Leave for 24 hours.

Peel the garlic and the ginger root and slice them both. Boil up the vinegar with the garlic, ginger root and all the spices. Wash the salt off all the vegetables and dry them. Pack them into a large sterile glass jar. Pour the vinegar and spices over them and seal the jar very tightly. Store for 6 months.

Pickled beetroots [V]

Total recipe: 600 kcal/24 g protein/negligible fat/134 g carbohydrate/34 g fibre

1.35 kg/3 lb small beetroots	*2 dried red chillis*
55 g/2 oz ginger root	*1 tsp black peppercorns*
1 head garlic	
1 l/1 pt 15 fl oz wine or cider	
vinegar	

Boil the unpeeled beetroots until they are tender. Leave to cool before peeling them and packing them into a large sterile glass jar. Peel and grate the ginger root, peel the garlic cloves and slice them in half. Add the ginger and garlic to the vinegar in a pan. Add the chillis and peppercorns. Bring the vinegar to the boil and then pour over the beetroot. Seal the jar tightly and store for 6 months.

Peppers pickled in olive oil   Ⓥ

Total recipe: 5330 kcal/6 g protein/582 g fat/19 g carbohydrate/
7 g fibre

2 red peppers	*1 tsp fresh thyme*
2 green peppers	*1 tsp fresh marjoram*
1 head garlic	*570 ml/1 pt olive oil*
sea salt	

Core and deseed the peppers and cut them into quarters. Peel the
cloves of garlic. Place the peppers and garlic in a bowl and sprinkle
with salt. Leave for 24 hours.

Wash the vegetables to remove the salt and dry them. Pack into
a sterile glass jar and sprinkle the herbs over them. Pour the olive
oil to cover the vegetables. Seal and store for 6 months.

Pickled apricots   Ⓥ

Total recipe: 885 kcal/27 g protein/negligible fat/207 g carbo-
hydrate/110 fibre

450 g/1 lb dried apricots	*1 tsp each:*
1 head garlic	*cloves*
1 l/1 pt 15 fl oz wine or cider	*black peppercorns*
vinegar	*green peppercorns*
1 tbsp allspice	*coriander*
	1 tsp sea salt

Soak the apricots in cold water for 24 hours.

Peel the garlic cloves. Drain the apricots and pack them into a
sterile glass jar with the garlic. Bring the vinegar to the boil with all
the spices and the salt. Pour the vinegar over the apricots and garlic.
Tightly seal the jar and store for 6 months.

ACKNOWLEDGMENTS

The recipes come from many sources which include classic French and Italian cooking. I am always in the debt of Elizabeth David and also her scholar successors, Jane Grigson and Claudia Roden. But there are other colleagues to whom I am grateful – especially Jocelyn Dimbleby, David Scott, Arabella Boxer and Natalie Hambro – for their cooking, though not always vegetarian, is full of imaginative ideas.

1986   CS

I am indebted to my wife for reading and commenting on the manuscript.

1986   TS

The publishers would like to acknowledge Peter Myers, who took the photographs, assisted by Neil Marsh, Mike Rose for art direction, Sue Russell for styling, and Jane Suthering for food preparation.

INDEX

Figures in *italics* refer to illustrations.

Other books in the Positive Health Guide series:

THE HIGH-FIBRE COOKBOOK
Recipes for Good Health
Pamela Westland
Introduction by Dr Denis Burkitt

DON'T FORGET FIBRE IN YOUR DIET
To help avoid many of our commonest diseases
Dr Denis Burkitt

THE SALT-FREE DIET BOOK
An appetizing way to help reduce high blood pressure
Dr Graham MacGregor

THE GLUTEN-FREE DIET BOOK
A guide to coeliac disease, dermatitis herpetiformis and gluten-free cookery
Dr Peter Rawcliffe and Ruth Rolph, SRD

DR ANDERSON'S HCF DIET
The new high-fibre, low-cholesterol way to keep slim and healthy
Dr James Anderson

THE ALLERGY DIET
How to overcome your food intolerance
Elizabeth Workman, SRD, Dr John Hunter and Dr Virginia Alun Jones

THE DIABETICS' DIET BOOK
A new high-fibre eating programme
Dr Jim Mann and the Oxford Dietetic Group

CHILDREN'S PROBLEMS
A parents' guide to understanding and tackling them
Dr Bryan Lask

KEEPING BABIES AND CHILDREN HEALTHY
A parents' practical handbook to common ailments
Dr Bernard Valman

THE HYPERACTIVE CHILD
A parents' guide
Dr Eric Taylor

BEAT HEART DISEASE
A cardiologist explains how you can help your heart and enjoy a healthier life
Prof Risteard Mulcahy

HIGH BLOOD PRESSURE
What it means for you, and how to control it
Dr Eoin O'Brien and Prof Kevin O'Malley

ASTHMA AND HAY FEVER
How to relieve wheezing and sneezing
Dr Allan Knight

THE DIABETICS' GET FIT BOOK
The complete home workout
Jacki Winter
Introduction by Dr Barbara Boucher